Poe Motion

Co Antrim Vol II

Edited by Claire Tupholme

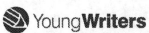 Young**Writers**

First published in Great Britain in 2004 by:
Young Writers
Remus House
Coltsfoot Drive
Peterborough
PE2 9JX
Telephone: 01733 890066
Website: www.youngwriters.co.uk

SB ISBN 1 84460 361 X

Foreword

This year, the Young Writers' 'Poetry In Motion' competition proudly presents a showcase of the best poetic talent selected from over 40,000 up-and-coming writers nationwide.

Young Writers was established in 1991 to promote the reading and writing of poetry within schools and to the youth of today. Our books nurture and inspire confidence in the ability of young writers and provide a snapshot of poems written in schools and at home by budding poets of the future.

The thought effort, imagination and hard work put into each poem impressed us all and the task of selecting poems was a difficult but nevertheless enjoyable experience.

We hope you are as pleased as we are with the final selection and that you and your family continue to be entertained with *Poetry In Motion Co Antrim Vol II* for many years to come.

Contents

David Bristow (12)	89
Keith Fulton (12)	90
Toni Vasey (12)	91
Stuart Brown (13)	92
Christopher Sung (12)	93
Neil Craig (11)	93
Steven McIlroy (11)	94
Sara Crockett (11)	95
Daniel Ross (12)	95
Caroline McCrystal (11)	96
Emma Scroggie (11)	97
Linzi Worthington (11)	97
Orla Doyle (11)	98
Christine Lynn (11)	98
Keith Mulholland (12)	99
Jonathan Gordon (12)	100
Mark Gillen (11)	101
Charlotte Cupples (11)	102
David Johnston (11)	103
Martin Galbraith (11)	103
Brogan O'Kane (12)	104
David Quaite (11)	104
Matthew Boyd (11)	105
Daniel McIlhagga (11)	105
George Dennison (12)	106
Clare Spence (11)	106
Adam Turtle (11)	107
Alison Ogilby (11)	107
Bronagh Gallagher (12)	108
Sarah Hamill (12)	108
Hannah Drennan (12)	109
Charles Deane (12)	110
Amy Millar (11)	111
Michael Byrne (11)	112
Rebecca Huston (11)	112
David Nesbitt (11)	113
Rachael Lightbody (11)	114
David Whann (12)	114
Catherine Dinsmore (11)	115
Jenalee Kennedy (11)	116
Andrew Scott (15)	116
Matthew Blair (11)	117

Robin Spencer (11)   117
James Scullion (11)   118
Abigail Nelson (11)   119
Emma McKay (11)   119
Lindsay Blair (11)   120
Michaela Gallagher (12)   121
Debbie Paul (11)   122
Sara Warwick (11)   123
Melissa McPeake (14)   123
Matthew Houston (12)   124
Andrew Laughlin (11)   125
JJ McAnally (15)   125
Robert Barr (11)   126
Sarah McDowell (11)   127
Jack Duffy (12)   128
Matthew McCall (11)   128
Steven Mairs (11)   129
Rachel Hamilton (16)   129
Adam Mackenzie (11)   130
Joanne Healy (14)   130
Amy-Ruth Morris (12)   131
Nicola Surgenor (11)   132
Linda Knox (17)   132
Joy Logan (12)   133
Julie Stevenson (13)   133
David Drummond (11)   134
Madison Graham (12)   134
Kristofer Galloway (11)   135
Andrew Logan (12)   135
Stephanie Smyth (12)   136
Thomas Clarke (11)   136
Anne Devlin (11)   137
Hollie Wilkinson (11)   138
Matthew McBride (11)   139
Alan MacPherson (11)   139
Andrew Swann (11)   140
Stephen Johnston (12)   140
Steven Orr (12)   141
Emma Small (11)   141
Adam Alexander (16)   142
Aimee McAfee (11)   142
Sheryl Weir (15)   143

Peter Coulter (15)	144
Beverley Boal (11)	144
Laura Erwin (16)	145
Hannah Moffett (11)	145
Samantha Stewart (17)	146
Vanessa Jackson (16)	147
Rachael Mckillen (11)	148
Samuel Steele (13)	148
Francesca O'Kane (14)	149
Jessica McAllister (12)	150
Jack Neeson (11)	151
Hannah Douglas (13)	152
Jonathan Holmes (12)	153
Louise Clarke (13)	154
Joann Andrews (13)	155
Ricky Andrew (13)	156
Sirene Watt (13)	156
Alexandria Stewart (13)	157
Kathy Michael (13)	158
Claire Hayes (12)	158
Grace Alexander (12)	159
Camille Delpy (11)	159
Andrina Elliott (11)	160
Glenn Kennedy (11)	160
Naomi Lamont (13)	161
Sarah Lamont (11)	161
James Burrows (12)	162
Judith Thompson (12)	162
Fiona Gibson (11)	163
Kirstie McKay (11)	163
Deborah Millar (11)	164
Stephanie Li (15)	164
Amy Stewart (11)	165
Christine Rock (11)	166

Cambridge House Grammar School

Rebecca Hall (11)	167
Diane Montgomery (12)	167
Stephanie Dowds (13)	168
Lauren Ferguson (11)	168
Jamie Craig (11)	169
Kathryn McWhirter (11)	169

Claire McIntosh (12)	170
Trevor Shiels (11)	171
Neil Davidson (12)	171
Emma Smith (13)	172
Mollie Arthur (13)	172
Jenny Bradley (12)	173
Steven Cooper (15)	174
Steven Herbison (14)	174
Mark Robinson (14)	175
Jill Surgenor (14)	175
Kathryn Watt (11)	176
Ellen McCartney (11)	176
Laura Bowman (15)	177
Sabrina Rodgers (11)	177
Aaron Osmer (14)	178
Diana Smyth (14)	178
Darren Rodgers (12)	179
Emma Magowan (13)	179
Lee Megaw (14)	180
Karen McQuillan (15)	180
Gary Worthington (11)	181
Lynsey McNeilly (14)	181
Jenna Fleck (11)	182
David Boyd (12)	182
Julie McCrory (11)	183
Josh Rea (12)	183
William Davidson (13)	184
Gary Bell (11)	184
Gemma Dornan (12)	185
Jonathan McKinney (11)	185
Emma McClintock (11)	186
Sara Kennedy (12)	186
Emily Hill (12)	187
Jill Robinson (12)	187
Lynsey Cathcart (13)	188
Ricky Smyth (14)	188
Aaron Crawford (14)	189
Adam McCready (13)	189
Stacey McAuley (14)	190
Peter Hughes (13)	191
Lorraine Frew (12)	192
Michael Blair (11)	192

The Poems

The Test

It was that faithful day,
It was the 11+ test today,
The daddy of all tests.

As I lay there in my bed,
I was shaking my head,
I didn't think I could do it.

My mum got me up,
Then came our pup,
Then I walked out of the house.

I stepped into school,
I felt like a fool,
When I saw everyone else.

I started the test,
I looked at the rest
And then I got stuck in.

I knew I had to have aid
To get this grade,
But now, there it was.

A big shiny 'A' grade.

Patrick McCrossan (11)
Aquinas Diocesan Grammar School

Horses

H orses are lovely animals
O wning a horse is a lot of work
R iding is a lot of fun
S ugar lumps are what horses like to eat
E very horse is different
S ummer is the best time to go riding.

Susan McSperrin (11)
Aquinas Diocesan Grammar School

Quickly

Quickly goes the racing car,
Quickly goes the dancing star,
Quickly the rain hits the ground,
As fast as we can run around.

Quickly goes the speeding boat,
Let's just hope it stays afloat.
Quickly melts the ice cream,
When it's caught in the sunbeam.

Quickly goes the motor car,
Around the corner very far.
Quickly the waves hit the sand,
As fast as the cheetah moves its hand.

Quickly goes the shooting star,
As fast as a speeding car.
But quickest of all is the spaceship,
Before it begins to fall.

Patrick Martin (11)
Aquinas Diocesan Grammar School

Sadly

Sadly the dead will never rise
Sadly the tears fall from our eyes
Sadly the blackness fills the skies
Sadly I'm lonely, me, myself and I.

Sadly the wind blows through the trees
Sadly the boats dock at the quays
Sadly we search but we cannot find
The love that is missing in our lives.

Rebekah O'Neill (11)
Aquinas Diocesan Grammar School

The Dark Night

It was a dark, eerie night and the only noise breaking the
solemn silence was the howling wind,
a sinister, luminous light shone down from the full moon,
the magic would come soon.
Far away in the distance a loud cackling echoed around
the empty streets and roads,
the voice came from out of the blue
and who owned it? No one knew.
A thumping noise answered the uncanny silence like the
footsteps of a giant,
the tree's pointy long fingers waggled and accused,
the magic folk had one night not to be abused.
Beware will you of that night,
because what happens can't be foreseen,
that's because that night, that night is Hallowe'en.

Siân Deighan (11)
Aquinas Diocesan Grammar School

A Riddle

I shine very bright,
Without a light.

I am yellow and pink
And don't need ink.

If I'm around,
I can always be found.

I make you blink
And seem to sink.

When I'm not here, you go to bed
And a moon takes my place instead.

Caroline McElroy (11)
Aquinas Diocesan Grammar School

Holidays

Holidays change your mind
In so many ways,
From the dull to the glaze
In a matter of days.

When summer comes,
It's all just fun,
Bathing and the shining sun,
I love to have fun.

Holidays put life together,
No matter what the weather.
It makes it even better,
If you have some friends.

Winter is a holiday
That is rarely gone,
But I go to ski,
Before the holiday is gone.

Michael Johnston (11)
Aquinas Diocesan Grammar School

Winter

W hen the wind howls across the land,
 I stop and think about the summer sand.
N othing is better than the summer sun,
 T here's nothing we can do now that the winter's begun,
 E very child wraps up tight,
 R eady for the cold winter's bite.

Shannon Cunningham (11)
Aquinas Diocesan Grammar School

The Wind

Some are in fear of me,
Some try to use me,
I can take apart a city,
Oh, what a pity.

At times I'm a gentle breeze,
You can walk with ease,
Or else I'm a twister
And I'll blow away your sister.

Sometimes I'm a hurricane,
That's when they choose a name,
I could be called George, Joe or Bob,
Then I'll ruin your job.

Why are you scared of me?
I'm harmless, can't you see?
I can't help all the things I do,
If you think, I'm less dangerous than you.

Conor Kerr (14)
Aquinas Diocesan Grammar School

Slowly . . .

Slowly the day turns into night,
Slowly the view is taken from sight,
Slowly the apple begins to rot,
Slowly we start to lose the plot.

Slowly the flower begins to wilt,
Slowly the tower starts to tilt,
Slowly the tree begins to grow,
Slowly but surely we'll all have to go . . .

Amy O'Kane (12)
Aquinas Diocesan Grammar School

I Am A Tree!

My branches are arms,
Waving in the wind,
People murder me,
Like they haven't sinned.

Some of us are hard,
Some of us are soft,
Some of us are furniture stuffed in the loft.

People stand beside me,
People start to eat,
Most people cut me down
And leave me in a heap.

Dead I lie,
Rotting on the floor,
Wondering what life would be like,
If I was a front door.

Ben McReynolds (13)
Aquinas Diocesan Grammar School

Cheerfully

Cheerfully the children walk to school,
Cheerfully the joker acts the fool,
Cheerfully the birds sing in the trees,
Cheerfully the babies touch their knees.

Cheerfully the flowers sway in the breeze,
Cheerfully the people walk at ease,
Cheerfully the children play in the sun,
Cheerfully everybody has lots of fun.

Maeve McQuillan (11)
Aquinas Diocesan Grammar School

Fire

Humans start me
Some like my heat
Some hate my heat
Some like my destruction
Some hate my destruction
I can't help my heat
I can't help my destruction

I hate being contained
In a lonely fireplace
Surrounded by bricks
Surrounded by stones
If only I could be out in the open
But not on my own
I would eat everything in my path

I am as hot as the sun
I am as evil as the Devil
I am as kind as an angel
I am as fast as a cheetah
I am as bright as a bulb

I have been here from the start
I will be here to the end
I could be the reason the humans meet their end.

Connor Lavery (13)
Aquinas Diocesan Grammar School

Brian

B rian is best of all boys,
R eally comical at times,
I always need to see him,
A lways fun to be around,
N o one's better than him.

Hannah Kerr (11)
Aquinas Diocesan Grammar School

Wind

I am the wind
Nobody likes me
People think I am cold and vicious
When really I am just lonely

When I am out on a summer's day
People just walk away
When I am having fun
People decide to run

This makes me angry
Which in turn makes me hungry
For the fear inside them
As I fly past their window
And send a shiver down their spine

I am the wind
I have a silver lining
I am always on the go
Trying to find someone I know

I am the wind.

Christopher Sisk (14)
Aquinas Diocesan Grammar School

The Metaphor Poem

He is a palm tree with leaves of green,
She is a warm and sandy beach,
He is a tall plant which grows beans,
She is a cold and slimy leech.

He is the fastest of race cars,
She is the one which comes last,
He is the round, red planet, Mars,
She is the crafty and clueless cast.

Sean O'Connor (12)
Aquinas Diocesan Grammar School

The Sea

I can be lots of fun for one person
A murderer for another
I can take lives in an instant
Or give precious memories of fun

In one place I can be calm
But in another throwing a ship in my waves
Sending its passengers
To a watery grave

I can be a vicious animal
Letting go of all my anger
But I can also be a thing of beauty
Under the warm sun
As children splash, swim and have fun

I am as blue as the deepest blue
Covering half the world
I am a monster
I am a friend
I am the sea.

Dermot Colton (13)
Aquinas Diocesan Grammar School

Quietly

Quietly the sun starts to rise,
Quietly the darkness dies,
Quietly the day starts off,
Quietly in the garden there flies a moth.

Quietly the streets start to fill,
Quietly the dew dries on the sill,
Quietly Mum wakes me up,
Quietly barks the little brown pup.

Garreth Brown (12)
Aquinas Diocesan Grammar School

Leaves

Leaves blowing in the air,
Clinging onto branches,
As if they were its hair.

Swept away by one big gush,
All brown and withered,
The leaves that once were lush.

Crunching on the forest floor,
Tramped by small children,
It's really very sore.

They are collected after they fall,
You give them to your teacher,
She hangs them on the wall.

People soon will not remember,
The beautiful crimson leaf,
They picked up in September.

Orla McLarnon (13)
Aquinas Diocesan Grammar School

Hallowe'en

Ghouls and monsters roam the night,
Horrendous beings give you a horrid fright.
Witches search to eat up children,
Skeletons tap dance around the street
And death comes to reap.
But the one thing the monsters hate,
Is when the cock crows and they've been up too late.

Shane McKee (11)
Aquinas Diocesan Grammar School

The Sea

I am the sea,
I roar and crash and foam,
But tire very soon,
I scare many people with my mighty roars,
But wash over their feet in a friendly way.

I am home to many scuttling crabs,
Who dig holes and homes in my sandy depths,
But I always enjoy
When people surf
On my turf.

I crash and sink ships against rocks,
Let people have a relaxing play in my gentle waves,
Some like to swim in my large foamy waves,
I stretch for miles,
As I am the sea!

Bronagh Rafferty (13)
Aquinas Diocesan Grammar School

The Sea

I hit the docks
I pound the rocks

I can be very angry
Or act kindly

I've been here throughout time
And don't intend to leave thy

A letter was named after me
What am I? Can you guess me?

Matthew McParland (11)
Aquinas Diocesan Grammar School

Chocolate

Mars bars and Milky Way
Never fail to make my day
Brown, creamy, rich and nutritious
Cadbury's chocolate is delicious
Lindt chocolate is very nice
It's just a shame about the price
But Belgian shells are my fave sweet
And I get them as a treat
PS, Mum likes them too.

Amy Hamill (12)
Aquinas Diocesan Grammar School

Solemnly

Solemnly a ghost comes out, creeping as it goes,
Solemnly the average bird gets scared by the crows.
Solemnly the Devil walks into the night,
Solemnly people stare at this disturbing sight.
Solemnly a fish swims up the stream,
Solemnly a girl dreams up these dreams.

Jack McConaghy (11)
Aquinas Diocesan Grammar School

The Storm

I can take out a building with just one shot,
I can wake a baby sleeping in a cot.
Ranting and raving, you can hear me for miles,
Blowing away trees and lots of roof tiles.
Loud streams of lightning and thunder I make
And plenty and plenty of lives I take.
Trees and leaves will go blowing away,
But, do not worry, I'm not here to stay.

Keith Lilly (12)
Aquinas Diocesan Grammar School

I Am A Tree!

I can be as tall as a giant
Or as small as a dwarf.
I can be as broad as a highway
Or as narrow as a country lane.

I can be as interesting as a film star
Or as boring as an accountant.
I can be as colourful as a sparkly dress
Or as dull as a grey suit.

I give shelter from the rain like an umbrella
And give shade from the sun like a parasol.
When the wind blows I sing and dance
And wave my arms.

In autumn I lose my character,
In winter I am bare and cold,
In spring I am reborn,
In summer I stand in all my glory.

Frances Greer (14)
Aquinas Diocesan Grammar School

Leaves

Summer leaves, bright green,
Swaying in the breeze,
Where they will stay until autumn comes
And gently fall off the trees.

From the arms of the trees they drop,
Waiting to float down,
Where they will lie all crunchy
And crumpled on the ground.

Autumn trees, red and brown,
Tumbling, tumbling, round and round,
Swirling and twirling down, down,
Until they reach the ground.

Monica Mullally (13)
Aquinas Diocesan Grammar School

The Party

Wake up feeling fine
Sunny morning
Day ahead
Mum says, 'Wake up sleepyhead'

Porridge eaten
I'm on the stairs
All dressed up
Going out soon

Phone rings, I pick it up
Sobs down the phone of
'Where's your mum?'

Mum shouts to me, 'Come on in
Gary's dead,' she says
Silently
'Pack your bags
We're going out soon'

In the car and
Travelling fast
No tears yet fallen
Nearly there
Dreading what we'll see
When we look at him

Next day
In his room
Pale white face
Staring back at me
Is it really him?
Lying on that bed
Or is it just a shadow of what
He used to be?

Sarah Early (11)
Aquinas Diocesan Grammar School

Silently

Silently slips the sandman
Soft-footed and slippery
Jack Frost is out tonight
Caressing the trees and grass
With his gentle, silent breath

Silently the moon slips behind the trees
The clouds, the moon
Whatever else would you want
The stars smiling down on you
As if they really give a care in the world

Silently the water moves
A whisper of long ago
Once in bed I thank the Lord
For all that is good and true
And wish that tomorrow is another different silent day.

Ciara Smyth (11)
Aquinas Diocesan Grammar School

Damhan's Hallowe'en Poem

H is for being happy at Hallowe'en
A is for the art that you use to carve the pumpkin
L is for laughing when you have a good time
L is for lots of sweets that you get for trick or treating
O is for 'ooooohhh' so scary
W is for witch that some people dress up as
E is for enjoying yourself
E is for effort that you put into parties
N is for nasty people that give you no sweets.

Damhan Farmer (11)
Aquinas Diocesan Grammar School

Autumn

Autumn leaves come tumbling down
Making a blanket on the ground
Red, yellow, gold and brown
Stand on them to hear the sound

Heavy winds to blow you clear
The winter nights are almost here
On the streets there's no one around
The warmth of summer can't be found

Hallowe'en is almost here
I just love that time of year
Herds of children flood the street
Screaming and shouting, 'Trick or treat!'

Tara Casey (11)
Aquinas Diocesan Grammar School

Casualty

I sit and watch the world go by
And listen to the children cry.
The lights and sounds and whitewashed walls,
Babies lying in their mothers' arms bawl.

I sit and watch the nurses hurrying,
Parents panicking, parents worrying.
The smells are strange but familiar,
Not like the ones at home, but similar.

I sit and watch the world go by
And listen to the children cry.

Bridget Molloy (11)
Aquinas Diocesan Grammar School

My Life

I float into the air,
Nearly bursting,
As I shakily think of past moments.

Flashing thoughts through my mind,
What happened in the past and right now,
Crossing the bridge to the other side.

Starting again as
Some memories touch my heart,
Leaving footprints as they go.

Passing through the rainbow
But stopping in time,
Although, sinking down deep into the water,
Then seeing the shore, the light.

Eimear Doyle (11)
Aquinas Diocesan Grammar School

The Seaside

The bright yellow sun beams down,
The cool blue sea leaks between my feet,
The warm, golden sand sticks to me as I stumble up the beach,
There are children splashing and playing in the sea,
People are screaming, shouting and laughing,
Beaming children run and skip to the parked ice cream van,
Behind them leaving clouds of dust and sand,
Families gather in the sand to make a sandcastle together,
Screeching seagulls fly overhead,
Children chase scuttling crabs in rock pools,
Jellyfish lie abandoned on the shore,
I can't help but wonder what could be more enjoyable than this?

Carol Doherty (11)
Aquinas Diocesan Grammar School

Down On The Beach

Sitting in class with my head down,
Trying to concentrate,
This isn't where I want to be.

I want to be down on that land of golden sugar,
With its glinting grains,
Each like a diamond set in gold.

Down where the sea laps against the shore,
Leaving its trademark of white frothy foam,
In a bubbling line.

Down where the jagged cliff,
Gilded with green, bears down on you,
Like an angry face.

Down where you can see the other side of the bay,
A translucent picture,
Like a memory.

Down where the sunset beams upon you,
Like a ball of fire,
Setting the sky ablaze

And then that piercing blue,
That softens that startling colour
And those tempting fluffy white clouds,
Like the pillows in my bed.

Like Heaven on Earth,
That's where I want to be.

Olivia Lucas (11)
Aquinas Diocesan Grammar School

Why Not Peace?

Human shelters torn apart,
As easily smashed as the human form.
Youth wasted in a sea of politics,
Age sighs, they've seen it before,
Wasted worry, the inevitable deaths,
Hunger and drought saturates the lands,
Mother Nature's growth worries away.
Beneath the pounding of the war song,
People dying, people crying,
Waiting for an absent relief.
A question mark pervades the land,
How can humanity destroy humanity?
Sorrow and blame spreads throughout,
As devastating as a plague.
Yet peace can exist in the hearts of man,
Sorrow and hatred ended.
Love can conquer all hearts,
Even those without pity.
How beautiful the world would be,
For every nation to embrace their fellow man,
To live without hatred,
Existing only to understand.
Listening to others' voices,
Hearing what they have to say.
Making space for all cultures, races and religions,
Seeing the human behind the belief.
One who feels the same as we,
Cries just as we do,
Bleeds as every human does
And loves when given the chance!

Emma Delaney (11)
Aquinas Diocesan Grammar School

Who Is She?

Dare I touch the surface of her skin?
Velvet and silky,
Delicate, milky.

Never underestimate her mood,
Because she could . . .
Raise her hackles into vicious curves,
Crinkled and rough,
Leathery tough.

She whispers to the wind on the wings of a gull,
Lapping and purring,
Echoing, murmuring.

Never underestimate mood,
Because she could . . .
In a temper raise her voice lashing out in anger,
Snarling and roaring,
Crashing, snoring.

When she's calm her eyes are the clearest blue,
Cool and inviting,
Calm, unexciting.

Never underestimate her mood,
Because she could . . .
Change her eyes to the darkest green,
Spitting and twisting,
Foaming, hissing.

She is the sea!

Eve Horner (13)
Aquinas Diocesan Grammar School

Silence

Silence falls around the world,
Silence in the air,
Silence in the atmosphere,
Silence everywhere.

Silence fills the country lane,
Silence in the street,
Silence in the village as the world falls into sleep.

Silence as the king he slumbers,
Silence as the seasons fall,
Silence as the stars all fall,
He is most silent, most silent of all,
The one who sleeps by the old brick wall.

Aoife-Rose O'Reilly (11)
Aquinas Diocesan Grammar School

I Am A Carpet!

It's so unfair, I can't be what I want to be,
Have to go where I'm told,
Cost a lot of money to be sold.

Oh, to be in a showroom,
You need to be cool
And made with wool,
But I'm just made with nylon,
Just a dirty old carpet to walk on.

Someday I'll be given a home,
Where I can call my own,
But then another day someone will take my job,
And I'll not be worth a few bob.

Natasha McNicholl (13)
Aquinas Diocesan Grammar School

Grass

In the wind, I am blown,
Treated with no respect.
Trampled on straight after sewn,
People make me look like a wreck.

Men and women play on me
And in turn they fall.
As spectators watch and see,
They run in chase of the ball.

I can grow very tall,
People have to weave through me.
Gardeners cut me so small,
To make their gardens look neat for people to see.

My colour is easily made,
Landscape artists should know,
They know everything about me including my 40th shade,
In the country I easily grow.

Farmers feed me to their animals,
It makes me very annoyed.
Those stupid mammals,
I try to grow away from those I want to avoid.

I hate the rain,
It soaks me through,
The rain is such a pain
And it's so true.

When it is wet,
I make people fall on their ass,
People hate me sometimes, I bet,
I am *grass.*

Matthew McAfee (13)
Aquinas Diocesan Grammar School

I Am A Tree

I am a tree,
With dark brown bark,
I move when it's windy,
My friends call me Mark.

People sit beside me,
Some fall asleep,
Others cut me down
And leave me in a heap.

They'll probably burn me,
Or leave me to rot away,
From the floor I look at other trees,
As they all stand and sway.

Soon they'll all be gone,
They'll all be on the floor,
They'll all know how I feel,
As I stand as a door.

As I stand as a door,
I look out the windows,
Wishing I could be out there,
Moving as the wind blows.

From the windows, I get a perfect view
Of the forest's morning dew,
There used to be one hundred trees,
Now there's only two.

Michael McCaffrey (13)
Aquinas Diocesan Grammar School

Grass

You think I'm all nice
All luscious and smooth
Green and brown while lying silent
I move only when the wind fights me
You think I love it when people stand on me
They say he'll be alright
I hate it really

Every so often my hair gets shaved
By a robot called 'Lawnmower'
It's like millions of knives going across our head
We all complain my friends and I
We bargain with the chief bushes to help us
But all they can do is nip people with their needles
It is really annoying

If I see them one day I know what I'll do, I'll grow them
And feed them and then cut them down
Just to see how they like it
The birds are our friends
They help us along
They take away the evil worms
That haunt us in our dreams

We'll be back, that's what I say
We'll be back to get you some day
So it's farewell for now but you'd better watch out
For I am grass.

Darragh Brownlee (13)
Aquinas Diocesan Grammar School

Water

I am water,
I calm you,
I scare you,
I can put you to sleep
And I can wake you up.

I keep you alive,
But I can kill you,
You could not survive
Without me.

I keep you clean,
Keep heat in your house,
Your body is made up of me
More than anything else.

I cover this planet's surface more than land,
Looking as clear as a crystal or as black as tar,
I am water.

Shaun Mulhern (14)
Aquinas Diocesan Grammar School

Fire

I am as hot as the sun
I can spoil everybody's fun
I can burn forests in my path
Touch me and you won't laugh
I can creep up without a sound
When water comes, I cannot be found
I am fire.

Matthew Maguire (14)
Aquinas Diocesan Grammar School

Who Am I?

Can you guess who I am?
If you can't, please be calm
I will tell you in a while
Please just listen to my case file

I am treated like dirt
Like a stain on that shirt
But when you need me
You do not even plea

I am your control centre
Yet, I am no mentor
Merely a guide to your TV
I am what you will never be

You are such a grouch
I always end up at the back of the couch
Living with dirt, as if I'm a waste
As if I don't have any taste

But see when you need me
Because I am your key
That is the time
When I am a slime
'Cause I use my force
To lose my source
To charge you money for batteries!

I am your remote control!

Ronan Tansey (13)
Aquinas Diocesan Grammar School

Shoes

Where we walk we cannot choose,
We don't ever get a rest,
We always have to look our best,
What are we?
We are school shoes.

We run, skip and jump,
We can never say no,
We are always on the go,
What are we?
We are trainers.

We come in different sizes
And different colours too,
All shades of blue,
What are we?
We are wellies.

We have heels or we are flat,
The trendiest award we will not win,
But you can wear us when you swim,
What are we?
We are sandals.

We are furry or we are fluffy,
You wear us at night,
But out of everybody's sight,
What are we?
We are slippers.

Rebecca Greer (14)
Aquinas Diocesan Grammar School

School

From Monday to Friday,
To start the day,
I walk to school,
With my friends along the way.

As I go into school,
I meet more of my friends,
With them by my side,
I don't care when it ends.

The classes I'm in
Are so much fun,
But time seems to fly
And to the next class I run.

By the end of the day,
I still wish I could stay,
Though it still means,
I can go outside and play.

Marion McGuigan (12)
Aquinas Diocesan Grammar School

The Sun

I can spread my love across many places,
I can put a smile on many faces,
With my arms, I push the rain,
I push it away, away down the drain,
Wherever you are, I'll always be there,
To show you tender, loving care,
No matter in wind, snow or hail,
I'll always appear on top of the scale,
You'll see me most in August or July,
But when it turns winter, I'll say bye-bye!

Claire Gunn (12)
Aquinas Diocesan Grammar School

Sadly

Sadly the miser walks along,
Sadly the choir sing the funeral song,
Sadly the old man thinks of years gone by,
Sadly the widow does nothing but cry.

Sadly the petals fall off the flower,
Sadly it gets colder hour by hour,
Sad are the rich - but saddest of all,
Is the poor man who knows he owns nothing at all.

Nicola Ferguson (12)
Aquinas Diocesan Grammar School

Sleep

I come upon all creatures
I lie them still
I am not of body, mind or spirit

I hold the mind in a grip of steel
The dark is my ally
I am obeyed by all
I am sleep.

Michael McKinney (13)
Aquinas Diocesan Grammar School

Skate

S trikers can move over, it's time for the skaters
K ick-flip the death gap, no problem
A ir-walk off the quarter pipe
T ail-slide down the rail
E nding with a 900 and landing on two wheels.

Ryan Magee (11)
Aquinas Diocesan Grammar School

Six Favourite Boys

Steven is my number 1
When I see him I go numb

Jason is my number 2
When he comes in, he lights up the room

Wacko is number 3
One day he will love me

Ryan is number 4
He makes me heat up even more

Darren is number 5
When I see him I come alive

Scott is number 6
He is the one that I'd pick.

Rachel Kirkwood (12)
Ashfield Girls' High School

The Night Is A Black Cat

The night is a black cat,
Prowling in the streets.
The stars, its eyes,
Rainclouds black like fur,
Prancing through the skies.

The night is a black cat,
The thunder rumbles as it circles its prey.
Lightning strikes! The chase is over.
Satisfied, it patrols till dawn.
The night is a black cat.

Elinor Stanley (12)
Ashfield Girls' High School

True Feelings!

I know I'm the one who made the mistake
I'm the one who caused our hearts to break
I'm the one who caused this mess
Now I must confess
My feelings were insecure
You loved me but I wasn't sure
It's taken me time to realise
That my decision wasn't wise
Now I'm sitting here all alone
Wondering if you're coming home
So here's the truth and how I really feel
I love you
And this time it's for real.

Samantha Patrick (14)
Ashfield Girls' High School

Summer Daydream

As I gazed up into the sky,
I watched the clouds float by.
All fluffy and white,
Like angel delight.

As the sunshine hurts my eyes,
I dream of further skies.
Where people live together,
Forever and ever.

As the birds hum and sing,
In the distance I hear the clock ding.
Oh! Where am I?
Oh! I'm back to reality.

Nadine Elliott (11)
Ashfield Girls' High School

Hockey Mad

I'm hockey mad,
I play all day!
I love to shoot
And play my way!

I love to run
As fast as wind
And pass to my best friend,
Emma Gordon.

I play midfield,
I love to score
All the goals
Off the floor.

On Monday night,
I play from 8 o'clock
Until 9 o'clock,
Then I take a break.

I can never wait
Until next Monday,
To play again
And win!

Rebecca Cupples (11)
Ashfield Girls' High School

Hallowe'en

Hallowe'en, it's that time
Children come out to rhyme
It's when ghosts
Play scary jokes
And witches fly high
To play in the sky
Hallowe'en will come and go
Next is Christmas, ho ho ho!

Jade McWilliams (12)
Ashfield Girls' High School

A Tragic Day

A tragic day
In late April
The new flowers' fragrance filling the air
Something awful happened
Me at the top of the stair
He fell
He rolled down, down until he stopped
My mind went blank
He was screaming
What would have happened if I went first?
Would I have fallen?
We drove to the hospital
He died
The funeral was sad
Everyone shed a tear
I am puzzled to this day, what if I went first?
That's what happened
One tragic day.

Rachael Newberry (12)
Ashfield Girls' High School

Ocean

On the ocean there is a boat
I wonder how it stays afloat?

Moving back, moving forth
Moving east, moving north

Bobbing up, bobbing down
Can you hear the ocean sound?

Fast approaching is the land
Green palms and golden sand.

Shannon Greer (11)
Ashfield Girls' High School

Conkers!

I raced to the tree
With joy and glee
To see what I could find for me
Saw something at the top
Thought would, could it be?
So I climbed and climbed
And got to the top
Saw it was huge brown conkers
I said, 'Whoa, let's pull them down'
So I pulled and pulled
But they didn't move
So I thought it's time to tug
So all of a sudden the tree broke
And I fell, so did the conkers
When I looked the ground was
Covered in huge brown conkers.

Nadia Given (12)
Ashfield Girls' High School

Hallowe'en

The sky is alight
With fireworks at night
Hallowe'en is so scary
Everybody is very wary
Pumpkin pies
Cats with big eyes
Witches, devils or a bat
Even you could be a cat
Trick or treat
Will you be at our street?

Julie Davidson (11)
Ashfield Girls' High School

Conkers

As I walk across the field to the big chestnut tree
If I look beside it, I can see conkers lying in a row
While children hit them to and fro
As I pick them up, I can smell autumn dampness
And moss as well
They're as smooth as paper and shiny as could be
They're brown and dark as they fall from the tree
Children search for them in their sight
To put on string to have a conker fight
Round one has begun as I give it a whack
Now my conker has a crack
As I start round two the conker has split
Soon it will fall to bits
It's now the third and final round
And now my conker falls sadly to the ground.

Lori-Anne Large (13)
Ashfield Girls' High School

Sandwiches

Bread, butter
Chicken and cheese
Mrs Dinsmore
What do you please?

Brown bread
White bread
Thick or thin
Drink it down with a bottle of gin

Buy the ingredients
Stuff them all in
Stay healthy
Except for the gin.

Chloe Milford (12)
Ashfield Girls' High School

Winter!

Winter is cold and chilly
When it starts to snow
Icicles hanging from treetops tall
With all leaves brown and falling to the ground
I hate getting up on cold winter mornings

Little robin redbreast searching for some food
But can't find it on the ground with the white fluffy snow
Poor little ducks can't swim in the pond
Because the water is frozen on a winter's morning.

Nikitta Anderson (11)
Ashfield Girls' High School

Ten Things Found In A Witch's Handbag

A witch's hat to show she's a witch
A witch's pet cat to sit on her broomstick
A witch's black wand to change a few things
And maybe there might be some magic black wings
A witch's black cloak to disguise her drink Coke!
A few little bats to frighten people away
That's what I think a witch keeps in her bag every day.

Lauren Stephens (12)
Ashfield Girls' High School

My Dog

Floppy ears
Cuddly to hold
Cuddles up to me at night
And is brown and white
It always needs a walk
And I think it tries to talk!

Jade Nicholl (12)
Ashfield Girls' High School

Keep Hoping

Blue leads to my love for you
Now you know my love is true
So when you're lonely, sad and blue
Remember I'll be there for you

As I lie there in my bed
All these thoughts rushing through my head
I lie there with my eyes wide open
I am wishing and hoping
That you will be here soon
So that together we can watch the beautiful full moon.

Michelle Steele (12)
Ashfield Girls' High School

Christmas

C hristmas trees glow
H olly hangs low
R eindeer fly
I cicles topple from the sky
S anta comes to call
T insel glistens
M rs Claus listens
A ll through the night the
S tars shine bright.

Leeanne Stewart (12)
Ashfield Girls' High School

The Lonely Dog

There was an old dog that walked down the street
It came over beside me and sat at my feet
Its fur on its back was tatty and black
It looked like an old potato sack.

Laura Brennan (12)
Ashfield Girls' High School

The Seasons

Winter is cold, a blazing cosy fire,
A snowy Christmas morning, beautiful to admire.

Spring is a newborn lamb, the sun begins to glow,
The animals come out to play, the flowers begin to grow.

Summer is a sunny day, an ice lolly nice and cool,
Everyone is happy now, relaxing by the pool

And finally it's autumn, the weather's getting cold,
The rain is coming back again, the wind is getting bold.

Melissa Brown (13)
Ashfield Girls' High School

Winter Leaves

This time of year, when you drive around,
You see the leaves change from green to brown.
They fall off the trees and lay all around,
Some land on rooftops and some on the ground.
You see autumn has arrived and colours turn bold,
Then the trees with no leaves will start to feel cold.

Kirsty Osborne (12)
Ashfield Girls' High School

Autumn

Autumn is here, the leaves are falling fast
Flowers are dying
Not long to last
Nights are getting longer
Mornings getting colder
Yet again I am one year older.

Lori Gardner (13)
Ashfield Girls' High School

Red!

Red is like
A furious fight
Something you do with all your might
Red is like
A trumpet noise
Outrageous and passionate
Red smells like a fragrant rose
Stronger than every other scent
Red feels like
A burning coal
Something you feel in your soul.

Leah Griffin (12)
Ashfield Girls' High School

Red!

Red is hot, loud and bold
This is a colour that is not cold
It swirls through your body when you are cross
It makes you want to twirl and toss
It seeps through your skin when you feel pain
It makes you want to go insane.

Joanna Rainey (12)
Ashfield Girls' High School

Blackberry Poem

As I pick the blackberries
They feel smooth and round
My hands are all red from the juice
They smell fresh and sweet
I can't wait to eat
The jam they will produce.

Natalie Edgar (12)
Ashfield Girls' High School

Falling Snow

Looking upon the sky
Seeing snow fall
Like white fluttering butterflies
Placing a white blanket
Upon the ground

Children's footsteps
Adults' footsteps
Imprints on the snow
Quickly covered up with
More blankets

The sky clears up
The street remains white
In the dreary moonlight
With all the butterflies
Flying home
With the stars sparkling
It remains silent.

Diane Priestly (12)
Ashfield Girls' High School

Autumn

Notice the autumn leaves,
Crispy brown,
Green and yellow,
Falling down,
Hear the rustling as you walk,
Savour the sounds - don't talk,
Sniff the fragrance,
Newly found,
Enjoy the experience,
While autumn's around.

Kim Armstrong (12)
Ashfield Girls' High School

What Is Pink?

Pink is the taste of candyfloss
Soft and sugary
Pink is like a soft teddy bear
Warm and cuddly
Pink smells like strawberry ice cream
Soft and cold
Pink is like fluffy dogs
Cute and snugly
Pink is like cute little baby girls
All dressed in pink
Pink is calm and relaxing
Pink is for love and passion
For the one you adore.

Elizabeth Mercer (13)
Ashfield Girls' High School

Child In The Dark

A silent room
A dimmed light
A child in the corner
Trembling with fright

The window's open
The door is ajar
A creak on the floorboard
The engine of a car

Suddenly a shriek
The rattle of a chain
Someone please help me
For my life's about to end.

Jennifer Louise McCallen (12)
Ashfield Girls' High School

Lost!

The night is dark and chilly
All is quiet
Not an animal in sight
Owls hooting from far above
Huge bushes moving from side to side
Branches breaking, falling on the ground
Craasshh!
My heart beats faster and faster
Pounding in my chest
Churning in my stomach
I look up into the black night sky
With bright glistening stars
Twinkling and sparkling far above
Like glitter in the sky
As I run
I can hear the wind moaning and groaning
I can feel it
Wrapping its arms around me
Hugging me like my mother
It gets cold
The morning light comes
The warm sun hits my face
The smell of the sweet flowers tells me I'll be home.

Jennifer Warke (14)
Ashfield Girls' High School

Mum

My mum is a soft ripple of chocolate,
She is a smooth gentle dolphin,
She is warm, cosy sunshine,
She smells like a sweet, fresh lemon,
She is a lively Monday morning.

Grace Thompson (13)
Ashfield Girls' High School

Rain

I went home
In my warm car,
I gazed out the window,
Watching people pass by,
Being soaked
By the rain.

The rain is
A beautiful sound,
As it hits
The windowpane,
Like music
To my ears.

I always loved a winter's night,
When raining out of doors,
Having a warm bath,
Coming down to sit,
In front of the fire
And having a nice warm,
Hot chocolate.

Dawn Blackstock (12)
Ashfield Girls' High School

Christmas Time!

Christmas time is full of fun
The tree's not up, let's get it done

Boys want skateboards, girls want dolls
Everyone's rushing to the malls

Santa's out and on the move
It's Christmas Eve, no time to lose

A present wrapped with a big red bow
Sitting beneath some mistletoe.

Sarah Ennis
Ashfield Girls' High School

The Blackbird

Strong and handsome
Proud and bold
Stalking the garden, in the cold
Creeping, pecking, searching for prey
He found a long earthworm
Then flew astray

His coat is black
As black as night
When he's in flight
What a glorious sight
Twisting, dipping and soaring high
The dark shadow in the sky.

Vanessa Ferguson (13)
Ashfield Girls' High School

Friends

As our days together are longer,
We both seemed to grow stronger,
Sharing secrets and stories,
Talking to each other all the time,
Running up our phone bills,
But knowing it's worth it,
Realising she's my best friend forever,
Having no idea what I'd do without her,
She's always been there for me day and night,
Sharing the laughter and the tears,
I know she'll be with me the rest of my years.

Victoria Maher (12)
Ashfield Girls' High School

If Classrooms Could Speak

If classrooms could speak,
imagine the chatter
The chalk would screech,
and the tables would jabber.
The board would boast
and the world map would mutter:
The floor would flinch because
Of all those dirty footprints
The text books would be
Screaming
'No more turning!'
Suddenly all is quiet
A teacher walks in quite tired
But delighted to see her favourite chair
Very old but sturdy
But the chair is quite
Different shouting
'Arghhhhhh!'
Not you please
Someone different
Now here comes the pen
Saying hello to its good friend
The class workbook
But it cries out, 'Please, no
Not more red pen!'
Then suddenly a blast from the door
The chairs cringe to see more of those
Terrible teenagers
Then all is quiet
Not a whisper to be heard
But the walls are talking
'What next?' they say.

Carrie Gillespie (14)
Ashfield Girls' High School

Spring

Smell of fresh blooming flowers
Sound of birds singing sweetly
Seeing bird eggs hatching

Watching newborn lambs
Finding their feet
Seeing children playing

Now winter's gone
Spring has begun
What a wonderful season.

Rachel Wallace (12)
Ashfield Girls' High School

Peace

Peace is . . .
A beautiful smile
A sign of happiness
Everyone wants to see
A world with no fighting
No racism, no war
Peace!

Kodi McBride (12)
Ashfield Girls' High School

Memories

Memories, memories everywhere
In my room and in my head
Good ones, sad ones
Funny ones too
Stuck in my mind like paper and glue.

Emma Mitchell (13)
Ashfield Girls' High School

Teenagers

I am a teenager
I don't like school
The holidays are short
But they are really cool

I am a teenager
What do you think?
Some teenagers
Smoke, steal and drink

I am a teenager
What do you think?
Staying out late
To play with our mates

I am a teenager
We're not that bad
Everyone thinks we are
And it drives me mad.

Jennifer Young (14)
Ashfield Girls' High School

The Seaside

I stand in the cool sea
As the waves hit my legs
Like a battering ram to a door
The heat bounces off my face

Waves lap over each other
As if they were pirates fighting for land
Soft sand beneath my feet and
A cool breeze gently passes by

Then, as if from nowhere
The wind gets stronger
Rain falls from the sky
It's now time to go home.

Megan Beattie (12)
Ashfield Girls' High School

The Present

Been waiting for this day
Has been delivered to my room
A box of delights
A big square box
Gold paper
Bright purple bow
I lift it up
Put it to my ear
No sound
No rattle
Carefully I take the paper off
The bow next
One hundred butterflies are fluttering about
In my belly a volcano is exploding
Tear paper carefully
The thing I wanted most
It's big, shiny, silver
Can you guess what it is?
A disco ball.

Hayley Murray (13)
Ashfield Girls' High School

Autumn

The rain bouncing off the window
The leaves falling from the trees
Rustling when walked on
The wind makes us almost fall over

Autumn
Close to winter
Nearly Christmas
Nights are darker
Getting colder

I love autumn.

Tara Brooks (13)
Ashfield Girls' High School

Dreams

Clouds as fluffy as poodles
Light white dogs floating around
Golden wings and halos on fluffy white dogs

White fields as pure as snow
Sprinkles of silver glitter
Covering fields of colour
Everything turning white and smooth
Clouds of cotton and baby-blue sky

White candyfloss beds with silver linings
Raining candy, floods of lemonade

A rocking chair next to a toadstool with a few
Sparks of pink, blue and yellow fairies!

A bird singing in a bare and beautiful tree
Animals roaming through the most wonderful forest
Ever to exist, full of blue, red and purple flowers
All the colours you could imagine
Dreams.

Alishia Corcoran (13)
Ashfield Girls' High School

Nature

Starry skies and butterflies
Moon shining bright as gold
Flowers standing tall and proud
As if a secret had been told . . .
Coloured flowers shouting aloud
Trees making faces in the shadows
Fluttering leaves, a bright red rose
A chirping little robin . . .

Joey Shek (12)
Ashfield Girls' High School

The Sky

The sky is blue in day,
It turns black at night,
You could lie for hours,
Watching the stars,
The white fluffy clouds,
As white as snow,
Watching them change shape,
Imagining what they could be.

Sitting in your house,
Watching the storm,
The lightning strikes,
The thunder clashes,
The rain bounces,
The sound is vicious,
It lasts for hours,
Eventually it changes,
The blue sky starts to show.

The summer arrives,
The sun shines through,
Leaving no clouds around,
I see the birds flying high,
Enjoying the summer sun.

The sky so high,
Is so relaxing,
It shows the season,
It shows the weather,
Look above and feel the freedom!

Kerry Carleton (12)
Ashfield Girls' High School

Stormy Night

Crash, boom, bang
A frightening noise
I'm trembling and shivering with fear
Scary and frightening is what it is
Sounds of a stormy night
Rumbling through the night

Hailstones
Massive lumps thundering down
I'm sitting trembling in a dark corner
Hailstones powerful every second
Then silence
God must have burst his beanbag

Suddenly another crash
Boom, bang
Then scary crackles when I am in my bed
Trembling with fear in my pyjamas

Bright lights beam through my windows
Stormy night stopping
Noises drifting away into the night
Getting silent every second
I'm glad the stormy night has gone.

Jordan Lemon (13)
Ashfield Girls' High School

Christmas Eve

Last minute shopping
Wrapping and rushing
Children skating, carollers singing
It's madness out there
But I don't really care
It's quiet in here
I've everything done
Thank goodness it comes only once a year.

Nadine Coote (14)
Ashfield Girls' High School

My Hobby

I rush home from school
And change my clothes,
No time to waste, to talk
Or pose.

I put on my boots,
Hat and gloves,
It's time to go
To the thing I love.

The saddle is on the girth
And the reins,
I'm all tacked up,
To go insane.

I mount my horse
And settle my feet,
Position my hat,
Ready to greet.

This proud animal stumbles,
As it moves on its way,
But recovers quickly,
To save the day.

I love the wind rushing by,
It's cold on my cheeks
And waters my eyes.

I can't describe
The way that I feel,
It could only be matched
By something not real.

It frees you completely
From worries and strife,
From mundane things
That are part of this life.

Horse riding's a hobby,
A love and a treat,
A way of life that you cannot beat.

Try it yourself,
I'm sure that you'll find,
Horse riding is fab
And will blow your mind!

Sarah Christie (13)
Ashfield Girls' High School

Winter

I am winter,
I come in December with my own atmosphere,
I bring dark and cold,
I make people dress up warmly with coats,
Hats, scarves and gloves,
I make the snow come down
And the wind swirl through the night,
On a winter's morning I make the grass,
Trees, cars, roads and buildings shine
With a thin layer of crispy frost.

Katrina Peters (14)
Ashfield Girls' High School

Orange

Orange is warm and soft
It's like the leaves falling off the trees in autumn
It's like a crunching noise
When you rustle through the leaves

Orange is a quiet colour
It's like a fire
On a cold autumn night
Blazing like the sun.

Kerry Murray (13)
Ashfield Girls' High School

Autumn Leaves

As the weather changes breezy
And the leaves change colours
They remind me of a golden sun
And dying embers from a fire
As leaves crunch under my feet
It sounds like I'm walking on
A bed of golden cereal flakes
They fall off the trees
As if someone is blowing them
This is how you tell it's
Autumn!

Emma McMurray (12)
Ashfield Girls' High School

The Life Of A Firework

O, to be a firework
And live in a ten second splendour
To rush up in the dark night sky
And explode with lots of colour
Looking down on the people below
As I go *wwwwoooo*
And that's the end of me.

Stephanie Meekins (14)
Ashfield Girls' High School

The Beautiful Garden

The beautiful garden so full of flowers,
I could sit there for hours and hours,
Flowers are neat, flowers are sweet,
But flowers aren't very good to eat.

Stacey Hamill (12)
Ashfield Girls' High School

Friendship

Friends are there to make you glad
Friends are there when you're sad
You turn to them for a helping hand
You have fun with them and always have
But friends fall out and that's a shame
And you only have yourself to blame
So make up, don't break up
And have fun for evermore

Friends are like warm pillows, lovely and cosy
You can tell them anything and almost everything
Don't lose your friends, you'll lose your faith
So hold on to them tight
Or you will cry yourself to sleep tonight.

Jodi Grimison (12)
Ashfield Girls' High School

Fireworks

Swirling, whirling, burning bright,
The fireworks light the dark, dark night.

Red and purple colours glow,
While children scream and shout, 'Yo ho.'

The rockets fly into the sky,
They boom and burst and gold sparks fly.

We stare agape, agog, asunder,
The noise, it sounds like lots of thunder.

The fiery smoke, what is it like?
I think it smells like Grandad's pipe

And now it's time to walk and roam,
All boys and girls they must go home.

Emma Hutchman (12)
Ashfield Girls' High School

The Dog

As he runs
He finds it fun

As he sleeps
Many secrets he keeps

As he runs to get his ball
He takes one great almighty fall

When he gets into our car
He stares right up at the stars

And now that he is here alone
He finds himself right at home.

Caryn Rutherford (11)
Ashfield Girls' High School

Cats

My cat means the world to me
My life was locked but she had the key!
If I ever feel lonely, she will be there
I hope she knows how much I care
She is a dream come true
When she is not around, I feel blue
Whenever I can, I squeeze her tight
Or else I can't get to sleep at night
I love cats and so should you
And that's a fact which is so true.

Ellen Keers (12)
Ashfield Girls' High School

About A Lake

The lake is so lovely
It is calmer than a sea
When the sun shines
It looks beautiful
When it hits the lake

It sparkles past a house
And past the beautiful autumn trees
In their changing colours of green
Orange, yellow and red

When it is time to go
It is disappointing
We would all like to see the lake again
But tomorrow we will.

Jade Morrow (12)
Ashfield Girls' High School

Autumn

Autumn is beautiful
The rustling leaves crunch as I walk
Red, brown, orange
Red like a strawberry
Brown like chocolate
Orange like the sun
When I reach home
I sit by the fire
It blazes beautiful colours that remind me
Of the autumn leaves.

Natalie Birch (13)
Ashfield Girls' High School

It's Christmas

I'm writing this rhyme
Because it's Christmas time
A time where each girl and boy
Is filled with great happiness and joy
Playing inside and out with presents and snow
Waiting for the cheers of Santa's great *'Ho ho ho!'*
Finally it has come, the best day of the year
Where we can all join together and celebrate Christmas in cheer.

Lindsay Gray (11)
Ashfield Girls' High School

Mitzi

My cat, Mitzi, is so soft,
She sometimes sneaks up to the loft.
She's never really, really bad
And always sucks up to my dad.
I think she's great and I love her so much,
She's never annoying or too much fuss.
So what I'm trying to tell you here
Is that Mitzi is so rare and dear.

Rebecca Yendall (11)
Ashfield Girls' High School

My Bad Friend

One day I went out to play
But my friend ran away
My friend is a little bit mad
And he is also very bad
When he runs away it makes me sad
Oh sometimes I wish I was a lad
But I'm a girl and I am glad
And I wouldn't make anyone sad.

Ashton Hood (11)
Ashfield Girls' High School

Hallowe'en

H allowe'en is here
A ll fireworks explode
L aughing and screaming
L ove is really what Hallowe'en is about
O h the joy
W e all enjoy
E ach second of Hallowe'en
E veryone does like Hallowe'en
N o one has ever hated Hallowe'en!

Caroline Thompson (11)
Ashfield Girls' High School

Tiger

Tiger, tiger, roar aloud
Tiger, tiger, scare a crowd

Tiger, tiger, eats its prey
Tiger, tiger, does it every day

Watch out!
Oh no, too late!

Tiger, tiger, got shot down
Now the tiger lies on the ground.

Alanna Blackmore (11)
Ashfield Girls' High School

Yellow

Yellow is the colour that shines so bright,
Yellow is the colour that sparkles at night,
Yellow is the colour of the stars,
Yellow is the colour that looks down from Mars,
Yellow is the colour of the sun,
Yellow is the colour that is so *fun!*

Alex Klisa (12)
Ashfield Girls' High School

School

Sometimes school can be so boring
Getting up early every morning
Standing at the bus stop with our friends
Discussing the events of our weekends

Going to maths first thing in the morning
Surely that's a devil's warning
Some teachers go on for ages
All there are, are excess pages

Soon comes break time, happy days!
Loads of fun in many ways
Back to classes once again
Oh back comes the suffering pain

Soon comes lunchtime, I'm hungry now
Some Pot Noodles flavoured chow
Off to locker to get my books
Off to English to read 'The Famous Cooks'

School has ended soon enough
Today has been extra tough
On the bus heading home
Playing games on my mobile phone.

Natalie Conner (12)
Ballyclare High School

My Team The Gunners

Arsenal is my team
Football is their game
Scoring goals is their scheme
Winning is their aim

Seamen is the keeper
He's great at saving goals
Henry scores with little trouble
He helped us win the double

Bergkamp is my idol
The 'Dutch Master' his nickname
Scoring goals is his claim to fame

So come on The Gunners, play the game
Let's fill the trophy cabinet
All over again!

Ryan Tweed (13)
Ballyclare High School

Goodbye

Goodbye is the hardest thing to say
I'll miss you and your love in every way
Oh please tell me what to do
I'm not complete without you

Goodbye always seems to come
But you're the one who made my heart go numb
Whatever happened to our love so strong?
You've made the nights so cold and long

Goodbye I said, now I wished I hadn't
You're now gone and my life has been saddened
So now I am saying goodbye
But please remember true love never dies.

Laura Wilson (12)
Ballyclare High School

A Dragon

If I were an artist
I would paint a portrait of a dragon

To do a proper job
I would use colours from every corner of the world

For his back
I would use a mountain range, all misty blue

For his boiling hot fire-breath
I would use poppies, tulips, sunflowers, all red and yellow

For his tail
I would use a silver-blue river winding through the Earth

For his skin
I would use the green landscape surrounding us each day

The world has much to offer
Use it wisely in every way.

Murray Dalzell (12)
Ballyclare High School

Autumn

Leaves are falling to the ground,
Swishing, swirling, round and round.
Red, yellow, orange and brown,
Not a green leaf to be found.

Hedgehogs start to hibernate,
Children are never seen up late.
Squirrels start to gather nuts,
Little ones build wooden huts.

Winter months are coming in,
Clocks go back one whole spin.
Nights get darker, days grow colder,
Autumn is here, we're one year older!

Alice McKeown (13)
Ballymena Academy

War

No matter where you look today
Everyone has only one thing to say
Did you hear there's a war over there
I for one, don't think that to be fair

We live our unruly lives
Whilst a poor person fights to survive
We take what we want not what we need
In these mixed-up lives we lead

People talk about terrorists
Have they found them? No, they haven't
They hijacked a plane and killed many
To catch them now will cost a pretty penny

Today it seems wars are about money
They don't care if they ruin a country
They bomb and attack but when they get flak
They say we're just getting them back

So this is the world we live in
Where morality and decency run thin
Where we say let's bomb them, it's faster
If this is our world, it is truly a disaster.

Ryan Moffatt (14)
Ballymena Academy

Darkness Of Clouds

Rolling clouds across the sky,
Fading now the evening's nigh,
Mottled shades no longer clearly seen,
But we remain aware of where they have been,
Light and dark move into space,
Dappled clouds create a race,
Majestic sky, night and day,
Filled with treasure, now gone astray.

Silk Hollingworth (11)
Ballymena Academy

You Won't See Anything If You Don't Look . . .

A weeping willow swaying dreamily in her woe,
A great majestic owl hooting all that she knows,
A diminutive field mouse scurrying among the barley,
A shrewd vixen slinking through the valley,
You won't see anything if you don't look . . .

A proud soaring eagle, gliding with the breeze,
A young dove fluttering slowly to freedom,
The sunrise on a dewy midsummer's morning,
The full moon glittering against the star bright sky,
You won't see anything if you don't look . . .

The unconditional supportive love of a friend,
A million fireworks embroidered into the quilt of the sky,
A loyal team forever standing at your side,
A glittering waterfall cascading to chilly fathoms,
You won't see anything if you don't look . . .

Shorsha O'Loan (14)
Ballymena Academy

Childhood

Whatever happened to those childhood days
Full of carefree play?
Nothing but opportunities to seize
And dreams that pleased
A land of peace
Free of worrying thoughts
Bursting with memories
That now seem so far
Such happy times they were
Making me content with me.

Annabell Glass (14)
Ballymena Academy

Shopping

Shopping, shopping, shopping
Oh how I love to shop
New Look, Tempest, FCUK
Are the places where I spend my Saturday

Miniskirts, leather jackets
Which never ever come in packets
Pointed shoes, fur-lined boots
When I'm seen, I get some 'hoots'

Faith, Shellys, Pod
Are the shoes I like a lot
Some I try, but never buy
When this happens I give a big sigh

Stop, stop, stop
Oh dear I have to stop
The shops are closed
I'd better go home, I suppose.

Rachel Simpson (14)
Ballymena Academy

Rugby

Oh, rugby is such a beautiful game,
The only bad part is the pain.
If you're a forward, you run about,
Rucking, tackling and throwing in the odd shout.

But if you're a back, you stand about,
Waiting for the ball,
When you get it, you run like mad
And hope that no one tries to maul you.

All in all it is a great game,
Full of hard hits, speed and skill
Which all can give your opponent
Quite a thrill.

Ross McKeown (13)
Ballymena Academy

Autumn

Red and yellow,
Orange and brown,
Are the colours of leaves,
Which fall to the ground.

Scarves and fleeces come out of the drawers,
Because it isn't summer no more.
Sneezing, sniffing, snuffling and coughing,
Are the sounds we hear each morning.

The sky goes grey,
The birds fly away.
Jack Frost comes out at night
And gives everyone a fright.

Autumn is here,
Summer seems so far away,
But it'll come back next year,
Well, I hope so anyway.

Johanna Barkley (13)
Ballymena Academy

Black

Black is the colour of a dark starry night
A chunk of coal burning bright
A lonely man's heart grim and sad
A withering flower ashen and dead

Black is the feeling of shame and sorrow
Black is a time like there's no tomorrow
Black are the tears of grief and fright
Black like a nightmare alive in the night

Black is hunger, black is fear
Black is knowing death is near
Black is heartache, black is never
Black is gone, left forever.

Christine McKay (13)
Ballymena Academy

Summer Holidays

The weather is warm
The sun always shines
And now my poem
Is starting to rhyme

Teenagers run and laugh and scream
Little ones eat large ice creams
Mums relax while dads aren't looking
Grannies come over to do the cooking

Amusement arcades are used a lot
Everything's great but has to be bought
Beaches are swarmed with young and old
Even when it is rather cold.

School is over
Time to play
Before the sun
Brings another day.

Gillian Chambers (14)
Ballymena Academy

Teachers

Teachers, that's the wrong thing to say
Going into some classes fills me with dismay
Don't get me wrong, some aren't that bad
It's just that some French teachers are really sad!

Teachers, that's the wrong thing to say
They must love it when they see their pay
Because spending a term with a disobedient year
It would be enough to make you turn to the beer!

Teachers, what a nice thing to say
Because it must be hard teaching 3A
Teachers, teachers, they know how to frown
But come half-three they're away like a hound!

Mark McCracken (14)
Ballymena Academy

An Autumn Wood

The leaves around me are swirling,
As the wind blows everywhere.
The sun is beating through the trees,
It gives me heat and protection.

I reach out to touch the oak tree,
The old, battered oak tree.
A piece of jagged metal,
Is how it feels to me

And how crisp the leaves are,
As I kick through them fiercely,
How fierce I must sound to them,
Like an angry lion hunting for its prey.

The crimson carpet of leaves,
Lets off a peaceful smell,
Just like that of the scent of a flower,
Growing up to be cut down.

Florence Kennedy (14)
Ballymena Academy

Winter Sea

A cold winter afternoon,
A brisk wind blows across my face,
Sand glides across the soft wet surface,
A wave collides with the sand
And some wild spray chills my face,
The sky is grey with cloud until it meets the sea,
The mountainous waves come crashing into rocks,
It's like a war of nature out at sea,
The sand dunes' grass blows from side to side,
The wind is fighting with everything,
As great gales blow around,
A small boat seeks shelter in the harbour's great walls
And angry waves pound on the walls.

Gareth Gracey (12)
Ballymena Academy

The Woman Next Door

There's a woman next door who's rather strange and odd,
She's really old and haggard with a black cat called Maud.
She keeps lots of peculiar jars in a rickety old store,
I think there's a witch living next door!

Now this woman next door, she always wears black,
Black skirt, black blouse or even a black mac!
She collects all kinds of things from a seashell to an apple core,
I think there's a witch living next door!

Moving on to Maud, you know the woman's black cat,
She's permanently by her side no matter what she's at.
The woman seems to have no friends which must be quite a bore,
I think there's a witch living next door!

The one time I was in her house, I did feel somewhat spooked,
Maybe the way it was curiously cold or was it the way it looked?
It had long, dense curtains and old, dank books which she
                                    seemed to adore,
I think there's a witch living next door!

If you look up close at this woman you might well get a fright,
Greasy hair and old chapped lips are not a pretty sight!
She's got cold green eyes and is getting wrinkles by the day,
                                    more and more,
I think there's a witch living next door!

It's October 31st, also known as Hallowe'en
And I got the proof I wanted, you'll not believe what I've seen,
I watched her take out her broom and take off from the floor!
Now I know there's a witch living next door!

Claire Headden (13)
Ballymena Academy

My Best Friend

Startled from beyond my dreams
Morning again or so it seems
My friend at last is fully charged
It has finally reached a full 4 bars

I hear a distinctive beeping sound
3 text messages I've found
The vibrant tones ring in my ear
Reminding me my friend is near

A peculiar language it does use
I think it dims my parents' views
It leaves them feeling infuriated
Or sometimes makes them so frustrated

Financially it seems excessive
And occasionally I feel possessive
I know without it I'd feel so lost
So I don't care about the cost

There's a multitude of things I could say
'Cause my friend's special in lots of ways
And in this poem a message I send
That my mobile phone is my best friend!

Vikki Worthington (13)
Ballymena Academy

Pollution

Wherever you look today,
You will see it everywhere,
You just can't help to stop and say,
That there is pollution in the air.

It is unavoidable nowadays,
'Cause it comes in many shapes and sizes,
This can be stopped in many ways,
But most people are just careless misers.

There is noise and air pollution and many more,
But any city in the world today,
The pollution level will continue to soar,
Therefore we must keep this at bay.

Children and adults alike can help,
But first of all we must create a plan of action,
This will have to include the cleaning of kelp
And many other conventions.

If everyone just did their part,
The world would have more breathing space,
When everybody makes a start,
The world will be a better place.

Ben Richardson (17)
Ballymena Academy

The Dark Horse

Like a black fiery Arab does the night come cantering in,
Luring you in,
Daring you to come,
It makes light fade,
Besieging you with the mysteries of many a year
For the dark is an unpredictable thing,
Just like a horse.

Like the airs above ground performed by a Lipizzaner stallion,
Sits the cycle moon,
Shining like the coat,
Of this stallion ready for show,
Kicking and bucking majestically, so high above the ground,
For the sky is an unpredictable thing,
Just like a horse.

Like a herd of Falabellas, reside the scintillating stars high up
in the sky,
Their iron shod hooves,
Ploughing the night,
Leaving indelible imprints in my memories,
Gradually making their way to their eternal mistress, the moon,
For the stars are unpredictable things,
Just like horses.

Like a thoroughbred bay galloping through the morning dew,
Comes the midnight train,
Crossing the divide,
Of night and morn,
Abandoning the darkness far behind, not to be seen,
He brings the light again to grace our eyes once more,
We start over, it is a new day,
For the new day is an unpredictable thing,
Just like a horse.

Rebekah Pedlow (13)
Ballymena Academy

War, Why Want It?

War, why want it?
It's shooting and killing that's it,
All the death just gives me a fit,
War, why want it?

War, why want it?
Guns, bombs, missiles and a knife,
It just gives families some strife,
War, why want it?

War, why want it?
Chemical warfare is just so rare,
Warfare is not fair, it's so unfair,
War, why want it?

War, why want it?
Biological warfare is the chicken's way out,
A bomb lands and you die before you can get out,
War, why want it?

War, why want it?
Generals sit eating and getting stout,
While their men get killed so just cut it out,
War, why want it?

War, why want it?
If we stand together we can stop this
And then we can get some well deserved bliss,
War, why want it?

David Boyd (13)
Ballymena Academy

The Romans

The Romans were a nasty bunch, they conquered far and near,
They came from Italy, but went away, inspiring fear.
They conquered Greece and Gaul, which now is known as France,
Romani saevi erant sed urbani erant.

The Romans were great engineers, their buildings, extravagant,
Many times they used a towering arch, the coliseum, it's giant.
They used these arches in via and aqua ducts,
Romani saevi erant sed urbani erant.

The Romans came to Britain and there they conquered clans,
But the Scotties wouldn't let them through, so they called on Hadrian,
To keep those Scotties well at bay, he built a sturdy wall.
Romani saevi erant sed urbani erant.

These beasts liked a lot of slaves, but they weren't cheap, you see,
So masters had to treat them well and not barbarically.
The worst off type of slaves must be those who worked in mines,
Romani saevi erant sed urbani erant.

Despite their feast of conquering, they couldn't take Ireland,
The Paddies fought them brave and true and defended their
homeland,
The Romans took just one legion, not enough you see,
Romani saevi erant sed urbani erant.

Thomas Dennison (14)
Ballymena Academy

The Cycle

Spring comes; the flowers flourish
Lambs prance and ewes glance,
Lots of rain, the sun to nourish,
Daffodils sway as in a dance.

The time is nigh and spring is by,
Summer's here for you and I.

The sun is high and the colours are bright,
Long is the day and short is night,
Bluebirds and sparrows will talk to each other,
They've flown their nest and left their mothers.

Autumn comes, rolling in with ease,
It sometimes can please but it strips the trees,
The colour is going, conkers will fall,
It seems so boring, but there'll be one for us all.

A shroud falls, winter is cold,
Freezing fingers slap and mould,
Light is far, no need for tan,
Just a smiling boy and big snowman!

The cycle spins on, unending, forever,
Continuing on, united, together.

Ronan O'Dornan (13)
Ballymena Academy

The World's End

Britain used to rule the world
Her soldiers always marching
Always fighting, always fighting
Her soldiers always marching

America conspires to rule the world
She has a back door to every country
Trailing Britain along in her stride
Her soldiers always marching

Britain's soldiers are fighting again
These soldiers are marching again
America holds her in their grasp
It looks like Britain is seeing the last

America has her axis of evil
Yet I don't see her name on that index of evil
America is the problem here
Whilst her people live in fear

Britain and America are led by corruption
Britain's PM doesn't have much gumption
Whilst America's President Bush
Is a cannon on the loose

Our leaders are primed
Fire, oil and industry are their drivers
Our people are blind
This is what I've found.

Richard Hynes (13)
Ballymena Academy

Being Me

It's not easy being me,
It seems like I've been cursed from the age of three,
I've been branded as a pest,
Apparently looking after me is a real patience test.

When I was only five,
That was when my bad side came alive,
Throwing stuff and messing up the place,
A glass broken over my brother's head was once the case.

At a door once I started throwing knives,
I'm lucky to still be alive,
Now do not laugh and do not sneer,
But this incident happened only last year.

Now you may be thinking, 'Oh what a bad boy,'
Throwing things and breaking my train set toy,
But good things I've done a fair amount,
Once I . . . oh no, that doesn't count.

My sister plays with my toys now but they're unclean,
But no wonder with all the places they've been,
She has one of my teddies named Blue,
Hopefully she won't throw him downstairs like I used to.

Now I've grown up and turned a new page,
Throwing and breaking things? I'm past that stage,
I have replaced my toys for a mobile and pager,
But what would you fear most, a baby or teenager?

Scott Thompson (13)
Ballymena Academy

A Day Off School

Imagine you woke up one day
To hear that school was off
'Captured by Martians from Planet Gray,'
Said the newsreader with a cough

Apparently they landed, last night in a UFO
Complaining loudly at the driver, who
Had flown right over Heathrow
Because he'd been at the loo!

Ah well, doesn't matter to me
I'm as free as a bird in a tree
I can play outside till teatime
Then come in and watch TV

I hope these Martians are here to stay
'Cause I could do with more days like today
With nothing to do but play, play, play
And no more homework to get in the way!

Iain Hamill (13)
Ballymena Academy

The Rugby Match

A massive airborne kick launches the game,
The teams follow up like charging elephants,
A ruck is formed,
Players dive into a sea of bodies,
Searching for the ball,
A scrum is like a giant spider eating its oval prey,
It wheels and heaves,
Conversions, penalties and drop goals,
Whirl through the sky,
Tries are the ultimate goal,
The victorious team is like a forest of cheering arms.

Charlie Simpson (11)
Ballymena Academy

A Poem About Timothy McVeigh

Sitting in a dark cell,
His mind is struck with fear.
Down his pale white cheek
Comes rolling down a tear.
His life scenes flash before him,
As he firmly bites his thumb.
For in his mind and heart he knows,
His end has almost come.

Soon his execution,
For sinfulness shall be paid
And he will now be taken,
After hours and hours he's prayed,
He now is being escorted,
A fear of life in Hell,
Has been written in the poem he left,
Sitting in his cell.

This man although a criminal,
In his poem has told,
He is the master of his own fate,
The captain of his soul.

Mark McNeill (13)
Ballymena Academy

On The Beach

Waves crashing on a beach,
A ball bouncing out of reach,
Children running on the sand,
Like a river flowing across the land.
Gannets flying through the spray,
In search of fish for lunch today.
They twist and turn and then they dive,
To take their prey by surprise.

All this action taking place,
As I walk along at my own pace.

Dayna Alexander (11)
Ballymena Academy

The Little Mouse

The little mouse,
He lives in a hole,
He hides from Dragon the cat,
Aw! The poor little soul.

When Dragon's away,
He will come out to play,
Or hunt for food,
The little mouse is in a happy mood.

He skips about the place,
With a huge smile on his face,
He hears something from the back,
Oh no! It's the cat.

In through the door,
Dragon comes,
He thinks to himself,
Where did he come from?

The mouse grabs his cheese cone
And is on his way,
He sees his home,
Yes! He's gonna be OK.

He dives through the door
And closes it tight,
Dragon tries to get in,
He pushes with great might.

Dragon hears a dish,
He's off for his fish,
Finally the mouse is left alone,
To eat his cheese cone.

Rachel Mark (13)
Ballymena Academy

Parents

I don't like parents because they are so mean,
They make you take a shower even if you are clean,
They never let you go for a cycle at night,
They always say *oh, you've got no headlight.*

I like my dad he's pretty much alright,
But if you get on his nerves he can be quite a fright,
My mum tells me what to do, she is *the boss*,
But when I don't do as she says, she gets far too cross,
Most of the time she's pretty cool,
But like I said she can be like a bull.

I'm always the one to get the snake fresh water,
Sometimes I wish we just hadn't bought her,
I'm always the one to give it a mouse,
My mum repays me by tidying up the house,
Even my room gets tidied, the whole house gets done in just one day,
Then when I go to bed that night I think, my mum, she's OK.

My dad lets on he doesn't like Spook,
He just stares at my dad with a real dumb look,
My dad is always the one who has to feed him
And after he eats, his breath is really grim,
See that cat, it's the greediest one I know,
All he does is eat and eat but never seems to grow,
That's what my dad always says when Spook walks into the room,
Then he jumps up beside my dad and gives himself a groom.

I have come to the conclusion that my parents are not so sad
And my dad and cat get on not too bad.

Marc Young (12)
Ballymena Academy

Desert Island

Lying on the beach, staring at the fish,
I wonder who I got here?
It is like Heaven on Earth,
With its gleaming sand.

Lots of lovely animals are wandering around,
Some white and some blue,
Every bird imaginable lives here,
Love bird, hens and parrots too.

In the sea there are lots of fish,
Each one darting about in the coral reef.
A dolphin jumps high in the air,
It lands in the water and disappears.

I hear a noise, it is like a door opening,
Help! someone is nudging me,
I turn around and look up,
It's my mum, time to wake up.

Laura Patterson (12)
Ballymena Academy

Trees In Winter

Black silhouettes against the sky,
Bare tangled branches way up high.
As they sway from side to side,
They still stand strong and tall with pride.
They had watched animals build their nests,
To hibernate and have some rest
And now as the winter is almost done
And the branches start fluttering in the sun.
It now becomes yet another spring
And all the birds come out to sing.
Soon baby animals will be born,
Thus the day that winter is torn.

Briony Wallace (11)
Ballymena Academy

Saturday Afternoons

Fashion items are what we are,
We wear labels from afar.
From miniskirts to skimpy tops,
We shop for these until we drop.

Trying on is our speciality,
Sometimes we forget about reality.
Clothes can make us very nifty,
But our mums remind us we must be thrifty.

To Quiz and NV we must trot,
But we must remember to keep the plot.
Around the shops we go again,
Picking up bargains there and then.

Oh how I love to shop down town,
It turns my frown upside down.
Every week we have lots of fun,
We shop until our money run's done!

Emma McIlveen (12)
Ballymena Academy

A Rugby Match

The ball soars in the air like an eagle
The opposition runs like a brutal herd of elephants
The crowd dance to the bagpipers
The anticipation is unbearable

The players run like lightning and score a try,
The crowd go wild,
The players celebrate,
The crowd is more relaxed.

The clock stops ticking,
The referee blows his whistle,
The players walk off the pitch,
The crowd applaud the team.

Nicholas Kinghan (12)
Ballymena Academy

The Search For A Smile

She was lonely and cold, she had nothing at all,
Nothing to protect her all but a shawl.

She wakes each day with a frown on her face,
No colour on her cheeks, she looks frail and weak.

No one to speak to, she lives alone,
All damp and horrid in her tattered old home.

She thought long and hard and decided with doubt,
She needed a smile and then she set out.

The search began for a smile of joy,
Like a playing girl or a playing boy.

She was getting old, her life had to end
But a weak, lonely heart was very hard to mend.

Sometime later she passed away,
Now she will never have another lonely day.

Ashleigh Thompson (12)
Ballymena Academy

Leaves In Motion

The movement of the leaves,
Bushes or the trees
Is quite a scary encounter
If you are alone,
It could be an animal,
The wind or a person,
The movement in the trees,
The bushes or the leaves
Is certainly something to be
Greatly admired,
Without the movement in the leaves,
There would be no point
In looking at the trees.

Gavin Kerr (11)
Ballymena Academy

My Favourite Things

I love to go shopping
For trousers and tops,
I go with my mum
And we walk round the shops.

I love to eat out
With family and friends
And go to the cinema
With them at weekends.

I love to go on holiday
Once or twice a year,
Go on big roller coasters
Without any fear.

I love to play sport
And go for a swim,
It helps me keep fit
And stay very slim.

I love to sit by the fire
And watch TV,
With a mug of hot chocolate
And the cat on my knee.

I love to play music,
To dance and to sing,
These are just a few
Of my favourite things.

Gemma Spence (12)
Ballymena Academy

Fog

It glided along in the breeze,
Making people sniff and sneeze,
Winter is coming some might say,
Others would just stay out of the way.

There it hovered over the grass,
Blocking people's view when they would pass,
Old ladies are driving so slowly,
How would they manage if it were snowy?

It twirled and swirled around the ports,
Making the timetables all out of sorts.
Oh dear the papers are late,
The financial advisors will just have to wait.

As the sun rises from its cosy bed of cloud,
A sigh of relief ripples from a crowd.
Everyone is glad the fog has gone,
Including my dog, which has found its bone.

I like the fog although it is cold,
I wonder will I when I'm old?
It is much better than the rain,
As it will quickly brighten again.

James Simpson (12)
Ballymena Academy

Fighting In The World Today

The fighting in the world today
I would pay to make it stop
But some day they will pay
Maybe at a drop
I hope it will all stop

People dying all around me
But nobody there to see them
All the wounds that people have
No one to care for them. How sad!
I still hope it will all stop

Police come to make it stop
But they just get hit
With missiles from the crowds
Of young people in the street
I really hope it will all stop

When they catch someone from the crowd
People just shout and scream
'You'll never get us'
And that is what it seems
Some day it will stop. *Please!*

Darran Norton (12)
Ballymena Academy

Hat-Trick

The two teams trotted onto the pitch with great pride,
Led by the captains who where both taking short strides,
On one side of the stadium was a sea of red and white,
It really was an amazing sight,
On the opposite side the stands were flooded with white and blue,
It really would have fascinated you.

The referee took his whistle from his pocket,
He blew it and the crowd's shouts were as loud as a rocket,
The blue team passed the ball about,
From the crowd you could still hear the shouts,
Then suddenly there was a massive roar,
The red team was about to score.

The red team's strikers was past the defenders,
Most of the players had surrendered,
He flicked the ball over the keeper's head
And the shouts got louder from the sea of red,
Five minutes later, once again, the striker was through,
There were screams from the crowd of blue.

He had the second goal of the game,
The other team's manager wanted to know his name,
Three minutes later he was on his own,
He scored this third and the goalkeeper groaned,
Two solo goals and a little flick,
This player had scored a hat-trick.

Rajan Bolon (12)
Ballymena Academy

Saturday Morning

What gets you up on a Saturday morning?

The alarm clock rings, adrenaline flows,
The thought of a match fills my head.
Excitement, exhilaration and anticipation,
All the emotions flood my mind.

It's a rush downstairs,
An energy-filled breakfast to consume.
Mum shouts, 'Hurry up!'
Dad yells, 'Come on, it's time to go!'

In the car Dad gives words of encouragement,
Sound advice for the match ahead.
'Remember tackle well and all the best!'
'Goodbye,' I say as I board the bus.

As we travel, excitement grows,
Nearer the pitch we go.
Excited chatter drowns the bus,
Boys planning clever tactics and throws.

We change and do our stretches,
Time for the match is fast approaching,
The coach gives his final words,
We carry his advice into the game.

We play through an hour,
Tackles, runs and tries, the final whistle blows.
We are delighted we have won,
Our efforts were not in vain.

It's that great game called rugby!

David Bristow (12)
Ballymena Academy

Supper

Drifting gently through the darkness;
Ready to jump out on its prey,
Comes the pale, cold figure of the hunter.

Gliding into the darkness,
Taking cover in the night air.
Here waits the predator, for its first victim.

He waits in the shadows,
Quiet he will be;
Soon he will unmask himself for someone to see

And out she steps,
Taking her one last breath,
Before her fatal death.

He swoops around her,
Grabbing her tight around the mouth;
Whilst sinking fangs deep into her shoulder.

The poison soon spread through her body
And she collapsed on the ground dead!
And there she lay, curled up in her death position.

The *vampire* knelt down beside the body
Sampling the freshly spilled blood;
Of a young eighteen-year-old girl!

Keith Fulton (12)
Ballymena Academy

A Teenage Disco

Flashing lights, music loud,
Bodies squirming in the crowd.
Voices loud, voices low,
Talking to someone they know.
Hair flicking, smiling eyes,
Looking round at all the guys.
There he is with all his mates,
Checking out the likely dates.
A little look, a shy smile,
Done in such a girlie style.
You look again in a while,
He nods and gives a little smile.
The music stops, the floor does clear,
Then you find him standing near.
When the music begins again,
You hear him say your name.
He asks if you would like to dance,
You follow him in a trance.
All too soon, the night it ends,
You say goodbye to your friends.
Now at home in your bed,
His first message you've just read.
You hold your phone oh so near,
For it holds his name and number dear.

Toni Vasey (12)
Ballymena Academy

Gone

He's standing alone on this hot summer's day,
The weather is fine but all is not well,
His great gran has died and he has to move on,
No matter how hard he tries his gran is still gone.

The sun still rises and it still shall fall,
But her voice shall no longer echo in the hall,
Her clothes are still here and her jewellery too, but
Without her they have nothing to do.

The rain will still fall and the wind still shall blow,
But she is now gone and this he does know,
The house where she lived still smells of perfume,
But he shall join her but it will not be soon.

The mountains still crumble and the waves still shall crash,
But no longer shall she drop her cigarette ash,
She is now gone and he is alone
And he wants her back even just to hear her groan.

The battle is lost and cancer has won,
His great gran is dead as if by a gun,
The killing was slow and boy did it show,
He shall have to be strong for now she is gone.

Stuart Brown (13)
Ballymena Academy

Chinese New Year

In February,
It's our Chinese New Year,
Everybody is happy and cheering,
To wish in a new year.

With traditional food and fireworks a-glowing,
It's red lucky envelopes with money a-flowing.
With lucky charms and good luck phrases,
Bringing in a Chinese New Year full of praises.

People are sweeping and cleaning in a hurry,
To get rid of last year's worry!
Cleaning the house from top to bottom,
To start afresh and full of promise.

With brand new clothes
And washed shiny hair,
The party's a-starting
And everyone is there.

Christopher Sung (12)
Ballymena Academy

Wind

Brilliant white sheets blowing gently on the line,
Leaves falling gently from the trees,
A few poppy seeds dropping,
Suddenly!
A strong gust of wind,
The sheets twisting around getting caught like fish in a net,
Colourful leaves scurrying along,
Trees bending - are they going to break?
Seeds move like machine gun bullets,
The wind dies,
All is peaceful again.

Neil Craig (11)
Ballymena Academy

The Terror Mouse

There was a little mouse,
Scurrying around the house,
It woke me up one night
And gave me a terrible fright.

As I lay there in my bed,
Scary thoughts were running through my head,
I thought there was a nasty thief,
About to cause us grief.

I shouted for my dad to come,
But as usual he sent my mum,
When I told her what was wrong,
She said I'd been watching television far too long.

When she started to laugh,
I thought that she was going daft,
How could she not be scared
Of the nasty thief I just heard?

She told me to take that look off my face,
The noise was coming from the roof space,
There was nobody strange in our house,
It was just a tiny little mouse.

Just that morning Dad had set a trap,
To try and catch that little chap,
Suddenly there was a *snap*
And so it seemed that that was that!

The mouse was dead,
I was safe in bed,
There was no need to worry,
So I fell asleep in a hurry!

Steven McIlroy (11)
Ballymena Academy

One Stormy Night

The wind was strong,
There was thunder and lightning,
The branches all swayed,
It really was frightening,
The hailstones and rain,
Did fall from the sky,
The rivers were flowing,
Their water was high,
The sea was rough,
The waves did roll,
The weight of the storm,
Really did take its toll,
But now all is calm
And now all is bright,
There was much damage,
After that one stormy night!

Sara Crockett (11)
Ballymena Academy

A Runner

Back break,
Heartache,
Limbs feel fake,
All for glory's sake

Spectators cheer
Opponents fear
Feel a tear
All for glory's sake

Heart rests
Did my best
What a test!
All for glory's sake.

Daniel Ross (12)
Ballymena Academy

The Iron Man!

An 'Iron Man' is on the hill,
He's falling now then all is still.

He finds his legs, his arms, his eyes,
The birds are flying in the skies.

The seagulls land upon the sand,
As he finds his mighty hand.

His feet had landed in a cave,
It looked just like a pirate grave.

The giant crawled to this rocky crevice,
In a style just like Elvis.

He picked up his feet and attached them tight,
He looked around it was nearly night.

He skipped up to the banks of the sea,
Something's missing but what can it be?

All is accounted for but one ear,
The machine steps out upon the pier.

He has a mission now to fulfil,
He disappears, then all is still!

Caroline McCrystal (11)
Ballymena Academy

A Witch's Brew

Take a pot as black as night
Take eye of newt and spleen of rat
Take spawn of frog and frog as well
Take spider's web and wing of bat

Take breath of spring
Take winter snow
Take haze of summer
Take blow of autumn

Take dark of night
Take light of day
Take the furthest star
Of the Milky Way

Simmer all together
By light of moon
On medium heat
And stir with spoon.

Emma Scroggie (11)
Ballymena Academy

I'm Still Here!

No one ever notices me when I'm standing right next to them,
It's as if I'm a brick wall which no one ever talks to.
Just once I'd like to be treated like a gem,
But it's as if no one ever notices me, like they don't have a clue.

If my family ever go out I'm usually forgotten,
When we meet someone we know, it's never me they stop to greet.
If I'm ever sitting down, no one ever notices me,
It's always someone else, it makes me frown.

Am I invisible? I ask myself,
Then people come and talk to me,
Why can't they just talk to me
Without me thinking I'm invisible?

Linzi Worthington (11)
Ballymena Academy

Windy Days

I hate windy days,
Where if you are outside you go numb with cold,
Or your cheeks and ears feel the ice cubes,
Then the rain starts and you get absolutely drenched,
Or if you look out of a window you see people's hair
Whipping around their face and their teeth chattering,
Or if it's raining you see pearl-like raindrops dripping off trees,
You see frantic women huddled up in their coats and
Old people crouching in the bus shelters,
If it's raining you feel freezing and heavy,
Yet if you look in someone's window and see them drinking a hot drink
Suddenly you feel roasting hot,
Or if you're inside and you see someone out in the rain
You feel like laughing even though you feel sorry for them,
Sometimes if the wind is really strong
You feel like it's pushing you forwards towards something,
I hate it when you're being pushed by a strong wind
And then it starts raining on you,
I *hate* windy days.

Orla Doyle (11)
Ballymena Academy

Have You Seen The Movement Of A . . .

Dancing hippo - bouncing around the stage
Flying elephant - gliding through the air
Skipping tiger - skipping quickly in gym class
Walking snail - walking through the streets
Climbing turtle - climbing up a mountain
Running butterfly- running the London Marathon
Skating dog - skating on a frozen lake
Swimming mouse - swimming across the ocean
Sliding cat - sliding down a slide
Parachuting monkey - flying in the sky.

Christine Lynn (11)
Ballymena Academy

Motion In Life

As a baby in a pushchair,
My mother took me everywhere.
However, in no time at all,
I had taught myself to crawl

And then before very long,
When my legs had gotten strong,
I walked, then ran and skipped about,
Rode my trike when we were out.

After a while I scrapped my trike
And moved on to a two-wheeled bike.
When my bike was old and done,
I saw a motorbike, it was the one.

When I bought a new sports car,
I drove it like a racing star.
A wife and kids stopped all that
And now I have a staid Passat.

Now that I am old and grey,
My grandchildren come to play.
I lean upon the garden gate,
As for me, it is too late.

Keith Mulholland (12)
Ballymena Academy

My Christmas Poem

Counting down the advent calendar,
Oh! I can't wait that long,
I wish it would come quicker,
The excitement will prolong.

The start of December,
But no snow yet,
It's freezing cold out here,
There'll be frost I bet.

Listen to the people,
Singing carols everywhere,
There's frost on the ground
And all the trees are bare.

Robins are chirping,
Staring in our window,
We're sitting round the fire,
With a warm red glow.

Crunching in the snow,
Throwing snowballs like mad,
Go inside all cold and soggy,
The pain in my hands, really bad.

Excitement in the air,
As it is Christmas Eve,
Santa will be coming,
Who knows what he'll leave?

Couldn't sleep that night (too excited),
Eyelids heavy like rock,
Climb out of bed, your head up,
Look at the clock.

9am!
Suddenly wide awake,
Look out the window,
At the frozen lake.

Put on a jacket,
Run downstairs like a shot,
Unwrap the presents,
Look what I've got!

Christmas dinner is ready,
The smell is divine,
Coke for the children
And for the adults, wine.

Don't forget the real meaning of Christmas,
When Jesus Christ was born,
On the first ever
Christmas morn.

Jonathan Gordon (12)
Ballymena Academy

Fire

Racing through the wilderness, destruction in its path,
Madness and mayhem in its aftermath,
It can be deadly as many of us know,
Terrorising countries, causing them much woe.
It cannot leave us alone,
It will burn at our every bone.
It destroys innocent living things,
None in its path escape the burning stings.

No one is safe from its flaming wrath,
If it continues racing down the burning path,
We will face destruction in our every home,
If we cannot stop it, it will destroy our every bone.
Log cabins, brick flats,
When it reaches these they'll be flooded with rats,
Pinching at leftover food,
But at our bones if it is in a bad mood.

We're lucky we have good protection and we pity those who don't,
They'll be burning with their homes, occasionally they won't,
If they aren't, they have fled to another place,
I just hope the fire won't give them a chase.

Mark Gillen (11)
Ballymena Academy

The Nightmare!

The moon was red,
That night of the walking dead.
The air was full of cries,
For he who doubts, often dies.

The worm in his head,
Twists and turns.
His soul like a cauldron burns.
His feet they trail like lead,
Yet his hunger must be fed.

The child sleeps with contented smile,
The figure at the window,
Is as sour as bile.
He'd walked the distance,
Mile after mile.
The window latch, it soon gave way,
The humans laughed - they'd all pay.

His hand latched onto her throat,
No time now for a submission note.
The muffled screams,
The pangs of death,
The innocence of a child,
Run through is mind,
Like an animal wild.

Suddenly his hand,
He gives a shake.
The child's eyes are wide –
It is awake.
The voice beneath carries up the stairs,
'Get out of bed!
Or you'll be late for Mrs Mairs!'

Charlotte Cupples (11)
Ballymena Academy

Star United

I play for Star United, a football team,
But to play for Man U is always my dream.

To start at the bottom is something I must do
And play in red instead of blue!

Our manager is Arthur and our coach is Ian,
On Wednesday and Friday we meet to train.

We train very hard and play lots of matches,
Sadly our keeper sometimes has few catches.

To win the McDonald's League is our greatest aim,
As last season's fifth was a bit of a shame;

But then in Carnlough things really improved,
From fifth to second we quickly moved.

We start the season with hopes standing high,
On Saturday we lost - at least we did try;

So to keep training hard is something I'll do
And play for the greatest, you know them, Man U!

David Johnston (11)
Ballymena Academy

Autumn

Leaves are falling dead,
Yellow, orange and red,
All the birds have fled,
Till spring bears go to bed.

Flowers look down and wilt away,
Through the wind, easy to sway,
Their pride will not decay,
They may grow back another day.

Corn collected in a mound,
Leaves covering the ground,
Rain making a defining sound,
Autumn is coming round.

Martin Galbraith (11)
Ballymena Academy

My Best Friend

My best friend is a shining yellow,
Like the sunset only brighter.

She is summer, only sunnier.

She is a field of rose petals,
Only a sweeter fragrance.

She is a cloudless sky
And brightens up the day.

She is a seventies babe,
Only more colourful.

A soft, warm, comfy bed.

She is a pop song, only livelier.

She is a juicy orange,
Just ripened.

But best of all she is:
My best friend!

Brogan O'Kane (12)
Ballymena Academy

December

December is the month of winter,
Happiness is all around,
With its soft and chilly breeze,
Happiness is all around.

Children playing in the snow,
Making snowmen, throwing snowballs.
Bells are ringing,
Hurrah! It's winter.

David Quaite (11)
Ballymena Academy

Christmas

On Christmas morning your eyes
Are as wide as mince pies
When you open a present
It feels very pleasant
Your Christmas tree is
Taller than me
You eat your turkey
And feel really perky
Your fire is as big
As Jesus' crib
Whenever you're sure
You drink lots of Shlöer
When your stockings are empty
You've got plenty
When you're out, you start to throw
Lots of balls of snow.

Matthew Boyd (11)
Ballymena Academy

Dusk

Dusk the drowsy time draws nigh,
A few twinkling stars enter the sky,
Everything peaceful, almost asleep,
The misty sky dreamy and deep,
A single leaf rustles the ground,
The slightest movement makes a sound,
Almost magical, peacefully alone
Is the overpowering moon,
Sitting on her throne,
The formation formed by the stars,
Bright lights a-roaring from Saturn and Mars,
It's so quiet, peaceful and still,
The time for magical happenings and charms,
Slowly dusk turns into night,
The beautiful time between dark and light.

Daniel McIlhagga (11)
Ballymena Academy

Rugby, Rugby, Rugby

Rugby is a brilliant game,
Although you get a lot of pain.

The only thing that gets me mad.
Is when the referee is bad.

It gets quite rough in a maul
And it's really good to get the ball.

I'm setting up to take a kick,
But I have to be rather quick.

When the forwards get in a ruck,
We all end up covered in muck.

When we get into the scrum,
'Crouch-hold-engage' we hum.

When we score the final try,
To the other side we say goodbye

And when we go home on the bus,
The winning team is always us!

George Dennison (12)
Ballymena Academy

Hallowe'en Mystery

It's Hallowe'en night,
We have the neighbours in a fright.
We knock on the door
Of number twenty-four,
Our pumpkins are hardly giving off any light,
It's as dark as a dungeon,
Should we give this door a gunging?
The handle of the door slowly turns,
Will we make their stomachs churn
False faces at the ready,
Will this fright be really deadly?

Clare Spence (11)
Ballymena Academy

Snowwoman!

People can't wait for snow
And yet they're glad when it's gone.
People love making snowmen,
But have you ever heard of a snowwoman?
This all started one very snowy afternoon,
In the middle of December,
We decided at lunch we would all make snowmen,
But one of the girls made a snowwoman.
They all laughed at her,
That night I had a dream about a snowwoman!
She was so round and perfect,
She said hello to me as though she knew me,
One week passed and nearly all the snow had gone,
I saw the snowwoman again,
She was sliding down the hill
And whispered to me,
'Don't forget me!'

Adam Turtle (11)
Ballymena Academy

My Heart And Brain

My heart is inside me,
I don't know about yours.
My heart tells me who to love or hate,
It knows all kinds of cures.

My brain is inside my head,
Nestled in between my ears.
It tells me how to read and write,
As I get on with the years.

Both these things inside me,
Help me to grow old and play.
All the feelings that are inside me,
Help me on my way.

Alison Ogilby (11)
Ballymena Academy

The Hunt

Jumping, jumping through the air,
Hooves thudding,
Dogs barking,
Birds flying up to the sky.

A fox running in a panic,
The horn blows, we're off,
Galloping up and down the hill
And over a ditch, round a tree,
Through a gate and flying across
A field of scattering sheep.

Smell of hot horses and hot riders,
Blowing in the wind,
Flying hooves and spraying mud,
The hounds racing off,
The scent was strong in the air.

Bronagh Gallagher (12)
Ballymena Academy

Alphabet

A would really like to see
B standing next to C
One below we come to D
He is standing next to E
On down the line is someone deaf
Well his real name is surely F
Here's G and H and I and J
That will lead us straight to K
L is like a precious gem
That shows the way to an M
On down the row there's N, O, P
Q and R plus S and T
Take a step down there's U and V
W and X are good to see
Y and Z, we're nearly done
It has been really good fun.

Sarah Hamill (12)
Ballymena Academy

The Price Of Liberty

Far across the ocean,
Live a race of things unknown,
Things seen only in your nightmares,
Things that are not flesh and bone.

They came to here and conquered,
Thus it stayed for many years,
That was a time of many evils,
Growing stronger on our fears.

And oh! how those fears were many,
How the people sat and wept,
Seeing cobwebs over doorways,
Gardens that were now unkempt.

But then there came a small rebellion,
In the form of a young child,
Born outside the reign of terror,
Where the land was harsh and wild;

It grew and swiftly came manhood
And a love for liberty,
He met a girl, who thought the same,
They wanted to be free!

So they travelled long and hard,
Until they faced the nightmare king
And though their force was nearly spent,
They battled with the thing!

At the news of the uprising, all the land had risen up
And had slain the evil garrison, as they sat down to sup.
But although it won them freedom, the price was very high,
A boy and girl lay pale and cold, both far too young to die.

Hannah Drennan (12)
Ballymena Academy

Space

I look out the window
And see the great black abyss.
Space.
Is there life there?
If the universe
Truly is infinite
It makes sense.
We are not
And probably never will be,
Sure about the matter.
After all,
We barely know much
About our own galaxy
And our theories don't make sense . . .

If there was nothing
Before the big bang,
How was it caused?
Some say the reaction of atoms,
But wouldn't that count as something there,
Before the big bang?
Ah . . . I see,
There was something there
Before the big bang.
A load of atoms you say,
Before the big bang.
Even though you said there was *nothing*
Before the big bang,
Can't answer that, can you?

Charles Deane (12)
Ballymena Academy

Music

Music isn't just bars and notes
And it isn't about soppy flowers and boats,
Music has different styles and types,
It all depends on what the person likes.

Let's take for example a boy who likes
Heavy chains and BMX bikes,
When he isn't listening to metal in the car,
He's dreamin' of rockin' the stage on his air guitar.

Then there's the type of girls who sing into their hairbrush
And when they think of their favourite boy band, they blush,
When they dance, they do loads of twirls,
They are classed as pop girly-girls.

If someone asked me,
I'd tell them my favourite would be
The reggae king, Sean Paul,
Who is the best of them all.
When I turn the volume up so loud it could kill
And then I put on 'Get Busy', I can't sit still!
I think Sean Paul is so class,
I'm definitely a reggae lass!

Amy Millar (11)
Ballymena Academy

Rugby

In my new school
Rugby rules and is cool
Football used to be the best
But now rugby beats all the rest

If I've had my Ulster fry
I hope it helps me score a try
When I am training
It always seems to be raining

Sit up, press up
Press up, sit up
Training can be very tough
Oh no, I've thrown the ball in the rough

Oh well I'm still learning
Still I can be yearning
To be the best
That will be my quest.

Michael Byrne (11)
Ballymena Academy

Hamsters

Happy hamsters eat
Tired hamsters sleep
Many of them sad
But some a little mad

Be careful they don't bite
Or your hand will look a sight
They are loved all round
And they hardly make a sound

Angry hamsters try to get out
While other hamsters sit and pout
Playful hamsters like to hide
While others like to ride
On their little wheels.

Rebecca Huston (11)
Ballymena Academy

Scaredy-Cat

When I was young
I knew a guy,
When he was scared
He would cry.

He was scared of
Everything,
He was even scared
When birds did sing.

He hated being
In the dark,
He loathed it when
A dog did bark.

He was scared
Of wasps and bees,
He was even scared
Of rustling leaves.

No one knew why
He had these fears
Of creatures, doors,
Flowers and beards.

People asked him questions
All through the day,
But he was scared
And wouldn't say.

He got so scared
He ran from them
And he was never
Seen again.

David Nesbitt (11)
Ballymena Academy

Love

Love is something special,
It's hard to describe,
Love is a roller coaster,
The biggest fairground ride.

Love is sweeter than sugar,
Fresher than the flowers,
Love is very precious,
Filled with golden hours.

Love is as deep as the sea
And wider than the galaxy,
It's like a growing family,
To live on for eternity.

God gave us love,
To be shared on Earth,
A gift from above,
For us all from birth.

Rachael Lightbody (11)
Ballymena Academy

Under The Bed

I always was scared of what was under the bed
Ghosts and goblins, strange things with no head
I always was sure there was something down there
But go down to see I never could dare

Every day I dread the night
Too afraid to turn out the light
Maybe someday I'll go down
And see under the bed, just what can there be?

But then the day came when I wanted to know
Under the bed I needed to go
When I bent down, a chill went up my spine
It was time to face this foe of mine.

David Whann (12)
Ballymena Academy

My Family

I hardly know just where to start,
There are quite a lot of us,
I only hope I can remember them all,
Without making too much fuss.

I'll start with Granny Peggy,
Because she lives so far away,
Sometimes she feels quite lonely,
So Dad brings her here to stay.

I love my granda Bertie,
Who is very kind to me
And so is my granny Kathleen,
Who often makes us tea.

There's uncle Jimmy and auntie Jo
And Christopher lives with them too,
They're all very fond of DIY,
There's nothing that they can't do.

There's Andy, Mandy and David,
Uncle Wallace, Margaret-Ann and Kaye,
But Emily is my favourite cousin,
She is so funny when she comes round to play.

Alistair, Rachel and Kieran,
Have gone to Australia to stay
And we have been to visit them,
Where we spent last Christmas Day.

But best of all there's Mum and Dad
And my brother I love so much,
My family are very important to me
And we will always keep in touch.

Catherine Dinsmore (11)
Ballymena Academy

My Dog

My dog is only four months old,
He likes to play all day,
The only thing he doesn't like,
Is when we go away.

He barks at all the strangers,
Or if anyone should come,
But at any other time of day,
He's just my little chum.

He has a little red collar,
That he does not really like
And loves to chase my brother,
When he is playing on his bike.

He is a little Border collie
And his coat is black and white,
When he hears a noise outside,
His ears always stand upright.

Jenalee Kennedy (11)
Ballymena Academy

Confusion

Without confusion, there is no questioning,
Without questioning, there are no answers.
Without answers, there can be no learning.
Without learning, there can be no teaching.
Without teaching, there is no understanding.
Without understanding, there is no knowledge.
Without knowledge, there is no soul.
Without a soul, there can be no love.
Without love, there is no life.

Andrew Scott (15)
Ballymena Academy

The Super Save

Running fast, sprinting through
Leaving them for dead
He's chasing back
He takes him down
Leaving all his teammates with an
Expressionless frown

The final round, the final minute
The final touch of the ball
It's all up to the keeper now
Standing strong and tall

The striker runs, strikes the ball
The keeper dives stretching long
He gets his fingertips to the ball
Forcing it to swerve wide
He may have his face in the muck
But he's triumphed over all.

Matthew Blair (11)
Ballymena Academy

Fear

Galloping ever closer,
A huge dark shadow that consumes all,
Pouncing on me like a panther,
Ready to rip me to shreds,
Concealing me beneath it like a huge cloak,
Torturing me,
Tearing me,
Killing me.
But then I kick the huge blanket off me,
Tearing it up into little pieces,
Stamping them into the ground,
The pieces are crawling away, defeated,
Crawling into the shadow, away from me,
I have done it, I have beaten fear!
But it will be back again . . .

Robin Spencer (11)
Ballymena Academy

In My Dreams

In my dreams sometimes it seems
That things are real to me
I've travelled back in time and space
In my nuclear time machine

When on the moon the man came out
To throw some cheese at me
And Martians aren't as green
As you and I believe they'd be

I stole the jewels from London Tower
And swapped them for some sweets
Now I've put on forty pounds
And can't get down the street

Some nights I dream of scoring goals
In the theatre of my dreams
And boxing is quite easy
When you fight a jellybean

Last night I dreamt I saw a chimp
Looking down at me
Then I awoke and realised
My mum was wakening me.

James Scullion (11)
Ballymena Academy

Cairndhu

Age-battered windows, blank, black and bleak,
Coldly they stare but no longer seek:
Overgrown gardens, moss-covered stones,
Sad wind through portals, sighs and groans.

Farewell, stately pride, your era long past -
Can such awe-inspiring magnificence last?
Exalted no more, but humbled instead;
Palatial nobility, lavish has fled.

Perhaps, in its dreams, it senses again
Silk-skirted ladies and grand gentlemen;
The unsuppressed laughter of children at play,
The hushed steps of servants at close of the day.

The glow from the windows, the flame within,
Silently, sadly, slowly grew dim:
It flickers no more, extinguished instead;
The age-hardened soul of the house is dead.

Abigail Nelson (11)
Ballymena Academy

Music To My Ears

I turn on the player and listen . . .
I close my eyes
I hear the beat of the music in my head
Thump, thump, thump it goes
As I listen to my favourite song

The words go whirling around in my head
Like the feeling when you go into a world of your own
And hear nothing but the sound you are thinking of

This is my world - only me
The music stops
I stop dreaming
I open my eyes
The song is over.

Emma McKay (11)
Ballymena Academy

The Haunting Ghost

It's coming to get you
It's here at last
You'd better be quick
You'd better be fast
Remember the last time
When it was here
The whole street
Was filled with fear

You cannot run
You cannot hide
From the thing
That's by your side
It haunts your body
It will make you scream
Tearing you up
It will seem

Are you scared?
Are you doomed?
It's building up
In every room
The thing that this
Happens to be
Is the ghost
That will make you flee.

Lindsay Blair (11)
Ballymena Academy

Cross-Country Race

Clippity, clippity, clop, clop
Up and over the ditch

The beats of hooves on grass
The pants of an exhausted horse

Round the tree and down the hill
Over the water ditch

Slackening pace, flying over the trap
Quickening again to climb up the slope

Sliding down the other side
Tripping as we go

Heaving and snorting, he launches
Over the fence with inches to spare

A crack of a whip
A pat on the shoulder

The end is in sight
My heart gives a leap

Over the last log
Down the last straight

Through the finish
Cheering all around

The gold cup is awaiting us
As I jump to the ground.

Michaela Gallagher (12)
Ballymena Academy

The Old Lady From Kells!

There is an old lady
Who gets on the bus each day,
She's never late, she's always there,
At 4.55 without delay.

She wraps her coat up tightly,
As she hobbles on the bus,
Pays her fare to the driver
And does not cause a fuss.

She doesn't push to get a seat,
She doesn't even try,
She just smiles and waves
At everyone she passes by.

She's the loving, caring sort of type,
Who would love to stand and yarn,
She never has a cross word
And would bear you no harm.

I feel sorry for that woman,
Every day on the bus,
Does she have a caring family?
Is she like us?

Debbie Paul (11)
Ballymena Academy

Hallowe'en Night

H aving a great time
A nd saying a rhyme
L ike trick or treat, smell my feet
L et me have something good to eat
O ut in the dark, dressed up as witches
W aiting outside in the dirty ditches
E ating all of the treats you have got
E veryone inside to get some pie
N ever knowing if they'd get the button or the money

N ine o'clock, it's still not dark
I mpatiently waiting for the fireworks to spark
G etting darker by the minute
H ere they go, one, two, three
T ogether we all watch them with laughter and glee

After visiting all of the houses
After seeing the fireworks rise
It's time to go and have a good sleep
So not another word or peep.

Sara Warwick (11)
Ballymena Academy

Love

Floating gracefully through a group of feathery, cumulous clouds,
Sweet voices singing in an harmonic chorus.
Vibrant colours flowers gently swaying in the summer breeze,
One single bluebird chirping happily to himself upon a
                                                    branch up high,
A young couple embracing underneath a baby-blue sky.

Melissa McPeake (14)
Ballymena Academy

Saturday Morning Torture

You have to go each Saturday
For rugby don't you know,
That's fine until half-past eight am,
'Oh Mum, do I have to go?'

This morning it was freezing cold
And wet as well, of course,
And all we puny first year lads
Are going to catch 'a dose'.

But off I went, brave as could be,
To face the scrums and throws,
Just as well Mum wasn't there,
She'd have made me blow my nose!

The shivering bodies gathered at the pitch -
No mercy were we shown,
But slowly I began to enjoy
And wondered why I had moaned.

'It was brill, Mum,' I said at last,
When the hour of fun was over
And even though I dread the thought,
I'll be back next week for more.

Matthew Houston (12)
Ballymena Academy

Autumn

Autumn has arrived at last
With the rain and stormy blast,
Colder nights and shorter days
No more sun's scorching rays.

Falling leaves, red and brown,
Make the gardener want to frown;
Hazelnuts and berries appear
Conkers fall, the children cheer!

People wrap up warm and snug
Farmers get their potatoes dug;
Apples, pears and damsons sweet
Rosehip syrup, what a treat!

Birds take shelter in their nests
Canada geese are our new guests;
Squirrels begin to store up food
Badgers lie dormant in the wood.

Andrew Laughlin (11)
Ballymena Academy

Snorkelling

The silence of excitement,
Stifled breath sharpens the senses.
A whole new world exposed in the solitude of an empty room.
Vibrant fleeting colours captured behind the delicate bubbles.
Telescoping views, a vision of the moment.
My lungs imploding,
I yearn for one last second the kaleidoscopic universe.
The silence of excitement will echo forever in my mind.

JJ McAnally (15)
Ballymena Academy

Our Country

The bomb and the bullet
I have never seen
But for nearly four decades
It has been

The destruction, the carnage
Is plain to see
Graveyards full of the RUC

People remembering
The dead from the wars
In Omagh Town
Killed without cause

The beliefs of others
Does collide
To create the problems
We feel inside

Every day I wake up
I wish it would end
So children could grow up
And everyone be friends.

Robert Barr (11)
Ballymena Academy

Excuses

It wasn't my fault you see, Miss
My clock hands stopped going round -
An elephant visited my house, Miss
And trampled it to the ground

The postman was chasing me, Miss
He says I ate his letter
I tried to dry my clothes, Miss
But I made them even wetter

They made me feed their cat, Miss
It hated me I can tell
They made me get the water, Miss
And snakes infested our well

My parrot told me a story, Miss
And it made me fall asleep
Just before I knew it, Miss
I was with sheep

So please don't blame me, Miss
It wasn't my fault you see
The whole world's just against me, Miss
Did I tell you I was stung by a bee?

Sarah McDowell (11)
Ballymena Academy

Friends

Friends are fun
Friends are cool
I have fun with friends at school

They cheer you up when you're down
They make you laugh and make you frown

They are helpful
They are nice
They're not cold and slippery
Like ice

They go to the cinema with you
And go swimming too

They have things in common with you
They hate it when you argue too

That's why friends are great.

Jack Duffy (12)
Ballymena Academy

Things I Hate

I hate winter
And I hate getting splinters.
I hate grapes
And people who wear capes.
I hate mice
And people who aren't nice.
I hate fat
And brown pussycats.
I hate crooks
And people who don't like books.
I hate wood
And people who aren't good.
I hate rats
And very ugly hats
And that's that.

Matthew McCall (11)
Ballymena Academy

The Haunted House

I opened the door
Into the hall,
I stepped on the floor
And heard a spooky call.
I walked up the stairs
And into a room,
A cold wind bristled my hairs,
I heard a big boom.
I went up to the attic,
Cobwebs hung from the beam,
Everything was static,
Nothing moving could be seen.
My torch moved round,
What's that - a bat?
A hideous sound,
It's only the cat.

Steven Mairs (11)
Ballymena Academy

Tree Thoughts

The whisper through the trees
The trickle of the stream
The birds singing merrily, for my sweet gain,
Insects buzzing hastily
The grass, the leaves
Is this not what I call home?
With the carpet of green, ever moving
And the ceiling of blue and white
To intrigue and enchant me -
The ever changing formations;
The painter's palette couldn't capture
The fluorescent vivacity of the buttercup
Nor the sharp bite of the nettle
No one can feel life unless they live it
And no one can live life without imagination.

Rachel Hamilton (16)
Ballymena Academy

The Game

I've saved up my money in pennies and pounds
For the game release of the final round
I dreamt about it every night
Of its sound effects and flashing light
My thumbs were twitching, I could not rest
I was sure this game would be the best
The way to get money was by doing the chores
I had to clean the car and scrub the floors
Monday morning, the day has finally come
I told my mum to remember the name
I gave her the money and went to school
I knew this game would be pretty cool
After school I got the bus
I knew this game would be a must
I opened the door very wide
Then my heart filled with pride
So I played it more and more
I'd completed it by the time
My mum came in the door.

Adam Mackenzie (11)
Ballymena Academy

The Big Day

Clenched teeth gating,
the dark cloud overhead.
Fingers defiantly disobeying,
breath - a conscious effort to control.
The calm, the poise.
The seconds evaporate loudly in my mind,
the sun breaks through.
A blanket of comfort
wraps me in the warmth of its rays.

Joanne Healy (14)
Ballymena Academy

My Special Place

The land of Ivory Coast,
Has a special place in my heart.
I could tell you of its weather . . .
The mighty thunderstorms,
Its raging lightning flashes,
The blazing sun and dusty grounds,
I could tell you of its animal . . .
The screeching hyraks;
The buzzing mosquitoes;
The dancing lizards;
The swaying elephants;
The smiling crocodiles;
The spitting cobra
And the darting deer.
I could tell you of its fruit . . .
The mouth-watering mangoes;
The perfumed Coeur de boeuf;
The sweet-tasting pineapples;
The juicy papaya;
I could tell you of its food . . .
The yams with pimento;
The peanut sauce with rice;
The hippo meat with vegetables
And all the spicy sauces.
I could tell you of the people . . .
The cheerful children who sing and dance;
The men sweating as they clear their fields;
The mothers cooking with their children on their backs.
This is my special place.

Amy-Ruth Morris (12)
Ballymena Academy

Autumn

As the seasons start to change
And the night creeps into day
Then green leaves begin to fade
As the summer passes away

The wind starts to blow
The leaves float gently around
Under the big oak tree
They fall slowly down

Leaves of different colours
Red, orange and golden-brown
Making a colourful carpet
As they lie on the ground

The trees look so bare now
As the leaves have now all gone
And the snowflakes start to fall
As winter comes along.

Nicola Surgenor (11)
Ballymena Academy

The Rainforest Tragedy

Stretching, reaching, fighting,
Unbreathing, just living,
The sensuous tree aches.
Crunchy rustle of the leaves,
Moistness in the cool breeze,
This Heaven oozes beauty,
Stands strong in dignity,
Before a chainsaw starts
And once again,
A paradise is torn apart.

Linda Knox (17)
Ballymena Academy

Harvest

The harvesters are out again,
To gather in the summer grain,
The leaves are turning brown and red;
'They'll soon fall off,' my granda said.
The days are getting very cold,
The sheep are resting in the fold,
The conkers, they are turning brown,
The spiky shells are falling down.
The hedgehogs now all go to bed,
Many trees you think look dead,
The frosty winds begin to blow,
Reminding you there might be snow.
We should thank the Lord our God,
For every little green pea pod;
God has blessed our land today,
Give our lives and Him repay.

Joy Logan (12)
Ballymena Academy

My Rabbit

I have a rabbit,
She likes to play
Just hopping and jumping
All through the day.

She is so active
Just running around,
So energetic
Just bouncing about.

She is so friendly
So furry and cute.
She is my rabbit,
I love her to bits.

Julie Stevenson (13)
Ballymena Academy

The Academy

I started the Academy,
Excited to see my friends.
We went into assembly,
Then sat on a bench,
The classes were called out,
Then we went to ours,
I made three new friends,
Adam, Adam and Peter,
We sat talking in class,
About some teachers,
When we went to our lockers,
David and I wanted to change,
Because he is so tall
And I'm so small,
Our last class was English,
Then our day was over,
What a relief!

David Drummond (11)
Ballymena Academy

Dolphins

They happily roam the ocean
With not a care in the world
They jump the waves like acrobats
As the waves ripple and curl.

Their happy noises echo
In an underwater land,
The ocean is their freedom,
Their capture is the sand.

Some people try to save them
They do the best they can,
These mammals are so special
Their biggest threat is man.

Madison Graham (12)
Ballymena Academy

My Favourite Sport

R acing is my favourite sport
A ction all day long
C hampionship cups if you're good
E very weekend
V alue for money
I enjoy the time with my friends
E lated feelings if you win
W orking hard to earn my pocket money

G oing go-karting as much as I can
O n my birthdays my parties are there

K arting all day long
A t the time trials
R acing to beat the clock
T en o'clock, lights out for raceview
I then have to go home
N ever mind, I'll be back
G oing with the pedal to the metal.

Kristofer Galloway (11)
Ballymena Academy

Different Speeds

Sometimes the waves move quite quickly,
The speed a tree grows is very slow,
Cars can go over one hundred miles an hour,
A lot quicker than a growing flower.

A magician must be quick with his hands,
A cheetah is much quicker than a man,
An Olympic runner needs to be fast
Or else he'll end up coming last.

Everything has its very own speed,
For that is the way that they were made.

Andrew Logan (12)
Ballymena Academy

Autumn

Autumn's my favourite month, did you know?
It makes me wear my big pink bow.
I think of leaves of every colour,
The brighter ones and even the duller
And when I go for a stroll outside,
I think of the leaves with oh such pride.
As they fall from the lovely trees,
They rattle and fistle like a bunch of keys.
I like to kick them with my feet
And make them dance all over the street.
The birds are singing, the trees they sway,
I just love autumn, 'tis true to say.
When autumn is over, I get very sad,
'Cause now it's winter and the weather gets bad.
So off with the pink bow, on with the coat,
Oh I wish I was heading for the sun in a great big boat.

Stephanie Smyth (12)
Ballymena Academy

Poetry In Motion

At the beach,
The sun shines like a giant flame in the sky,
The seagulls fly past like planes at an airport,
The waves come in like tigers pouncing on their prey.
The cool breeze blows like a fan in an office,
The children run about like bulls in china shops.
The tourists eat like packs of wolves,
The people swim like corks floating on the water.
The kites flutter like sheets on a clothes line,
The boats sail like swans on a lake,
The parents laugh like a group of hyenas.

Thomas Clarke (11)
Ballymena Academy

The Crash!

The train was along at 99 miles per hour,
Then came a thunderous rain shower.
The tracks became slippy,
The train slipped off onto the grassy bank
And went sliding and slipping along.

There was a loud bang,
The train had tipped over
And everyone sang,
Argh!
The young woman beside me got out her mobile
And rang for help to save us all!

After a while we heard sirens whirl
And the reflection of flashing lights.
It was getting dark now,
Help was almost here,
Oh! not such a wonderful day!

Help was here,
I could hear men slamming doors,
I could see ambulances, police cars
And the fire brigade,
Oh! help is here, it might be a wonderful day!

Anne Devlin (11)
Ballymena Academy

Books

Books are great, books are fun,
Lots to do for everyone.

History books are really good,
They tell you all about the feuds.

Wildlife books interest me,
They tell you about the birds and the bees.

Some books frighten me,
They're really not meant to be.

Fiction books are the best,
They really do beat the rest.

Some books are not good,
They might get me in a mood.

As I read my book each night,
It makes me feel really bright.

I don't want to start a debate,
It's just that I think books are *great!*

Hollie Wilkinson (11)
Ballymena Academy

It!

There was a little monster living in my house,
Soft and warm and fuzzy but as ugly as a louse.
I saw it on the ceiling, I saw it on the floor,
The next time I saw it, it had climbed onto a door.

I opened up the cupboard and guess what was in store?
There was the little monster, 'That's it!' I screamed. 'No more.'

I found it on my favourite chair,
It was even clinging to my hair.
I shook and shivered but it wouldn't go,
The stupid little so and so!

It jumped from my hair and fell on my bed,
At first I thought that it was dead.
I gazed upon its little face,
Then decided it was really ace.

The chase was over and it became my friend,
Thank goodness the torture was at an end.
At last it was no longer it!
It was my very best pal, Kit.

Matthew McBride (11)
Ballymena Academy

Tiger

T error touches their hearts as
I nto the clearing he glides,
G raceful, glorious in his silence
E vening has brought his dreaded visit,
R uler of the jungle world.

Alan MacPherson (11)
Ballymena Academy

This

This goes fast when you want it to go slow,
This goes slow when you want it to go fast,
This brings a new season
And a new day.

This makes the leaves
Fall from the trees,
This is why everyone
Grows so old.

This is why
The clock face changes,
This is why
Wallpaper fades.

This is why
So many things rot,
This is
Time.

Andrew Swann (11)
Ballymena Academy

Troubled Waters

I sit at my bedroom window,
A dazzling bolt of lightning illuminates the dark sky.
The thunder roars
And the waves crash against the jagged rocks,
Swelling as if an underwater monster is about to emerge.
A boat is torn apart as the sea swirls around it
And the wind blows rain into the faces of bystanders.
I'm glad I'm inside - sheltered and safe.

Stephen Johnston (12)
Ballymena Academy

School's Such A Bore

Almost every kid hates school
Having to get up early
Wearing those goofy uniforms
Learning algebra and other things that we don't even need

Most people would rather be at home watching TV
Or be out playing football
Our parents say enjoy it
They say it's the best days of our lives

If school wasn't invented
We would never have TVs
Or computers or even mobile phones
Because no one would be smart enough to invent them

Even though it's boring
School isn't all bad
And if you hate it so much
You can leave after 14 years.

Steven Orr (12)
Ballymena Academy

Trees In Autumn

Trees in autumn, how their colours have changed,
For now their green has turned red with rage.
The wind blows past the trees' sturdy boughs
And swirls their leaves up into the clouds.

Leaves keep on falling and tumbling down,
Creating a carpet of golden-brown,
Now that the trees' branches are almost bare,
The birds are starting to fly off, with care

And as the days get dark sooner each night,
The trees' branches still keep swaying in the moonlight,
From the tips of their branches to their roots down below,
Soon they will all be wiped out with snow.

Emma Small (11)
Ballymena Academy

Tears

Tears roll down her face
Tears of sorrow inflicted
I must take her from this place
Get the perpetrators convicted

The sparkle in her eye is gone
A battle that can never be won
The lightheartedness in her voice
Has left her, but not by choice

I have to fight, I have to try
To stop whatever makes her cry
To take her from this evil place
To keep the tears from her face

Tears roll down her face
Tears of sorrow inflicted
I must take her from this place
Get the perpetrators convicted.

Adam Alexander (16)
Ballymena Academy

As Beautiful As A Cloud

She floats around the light blue sky,
Like a big ball of white fluff.

Her gentle whisper drifts through the air
And tickles your ear like the touch of a hair.

Although she hides the sun,
She makes it like an iced bun.

She adds colour to the boring blue,
With a splash of pure white.

But when she cries,
Which often happens,
Her perfect teardrops shower the Earth.

Aimee McAfee (11)
Ballymena Academy

Colours Of The Countryside!

As the bus went jolting along the old, grey, dusty road,
The brightness of the sun shone yellow streaks through
the bus window.
As I stepped off the bus I could smell the scent of the freshly
cut, green grass,
And I could see the new baby lambs in their beautiful white coats,
Leaping and springing high into the background of the blue sky.

Then as I walked on down the grey road,
Past the old, brown, derelict farmhouse with the cracked,
brown roof tiles covered in green moss,
And the garden with the purple thistles leaning up against
the rustic gate
And the wild red poppies on the ditch.

There was also a sea of wild white snowdrops below the
old apple trees,
I picked a green apple off the tree and headed towards my
house with the beige brick pillars,
When I reached my black front door with the big, gold handle,
I unlocked the door with my shiny, silver key and stepped inside.

It was so pleasant to see the glowing orange fire lit,
And I fell asleep that night on my navy leather sofa;
After drinking a cup of creamy coffee.

Sheryl Weir (15)
Ballymena Academy

Learn To Forget

Hatred, war and despair
The world is quite a place
Starvation, death and anger
Staring us in the face

People do not care
Despite what they're told
Leaving people homeless
In the bitter cold

War is on the agenda
While needs are left behind
Yet the government often say
We have other things on our mind

The saying tends to go
Clearly written in bold
'Learn to forget'
Or so I've been told.

Peter Coulter (15)
Ballymena Academy

Galloping At Night

Galloping in the middle of the night,
Hair streaming in the moonlight,
Going as fast as the wind in a gale,
Nobody to see them and tell the tale.

On the hills, the moon lit up,
A ghostly figure, horse and pup,
Nothing to disturb the stillness,
But the puppy's barks about his sleepiness.

A steady rhythm of the horse's hooves,
The only sound, the only moves,
As they galloped out of sight,
Only animals saw them gallop in the night.

Beverley Boal (11)
Ballymena Academy

Final Steps

I'm one step closer to my ultimate nightmare,
A corridor of savage beasts,
Standing in shadows without a care,
Until along comes their next feast.

Do I dare to enter this dark cave?
Do I stride on to meet my fate?
If I enter I will surely meet my grave,
Even now it may be too late.

Standing tall I begin to prepare,
They turn to face their opposition,
Their claws are ready to tear,
But I'm ready to put them in their position.

All my fear has been drained,
Now I am nearly done,
So much confidence has been gained
And the battle finally won.

Laura Erwin (16)
Ballymena Academy

I Saw Someone Running

I saw someone running the other day,
He was running fast and steady when he passed my way.
He was running like a great hare,
An old man down the street shouted,
'Hey, watch! Have some care.'
Then he started to slow down,
His heart was beating, his face a nasty frown,
By this time he was going the speed of a snail,
His sweaty T-shirt looked as if someone had just thrown at
                                    him a water pail.
I looked at him, he looked at me,
That was the end, I ran as quick as a buzzing bee.

Hannah Moffett (11)
Ballymena Academy

Learning The Hard Lesson

I'm all grown up now, I'm leaving soon,
Not much left to do here,
Exams to pass . . . or maybe not.

My life has been spent sailing through,
With minimal work, hoping for the best.
Giving my all . . . or maybe not.

Images I see on TV or in books,
Of people I hope one day to be.
My glorious future . . . or maybe not.

Friends give me strength to try harder now,
Showing me how to carry on.
I'll do better . . . or maybe not.

6am, up and shower to get ready,
Ready for a job I don't enjoy.
I did my best . . . or maybe not.

Looking back I see, in hindsight,
The path not taken, much considered.
I've learned my lesson.

Samantha Stewart (17)
Ballymena Academy

Life In A Box

Be still, oh rippling river,
Silver creases of silk clothing the air from below;
Be soft, oh wailers on the wind,
Stir not your pitch to prick an ear.
Be changeless, chrysalis; unborn babe unbirthed,
Write not to enter a weary world,
Live not, feel not, change not -

For to live, is to exist
As a silenus whose innards contradict their case,
For outer coatings erode with time,
While inner being remains unspoiled.
Be changeless, soul, for living man still mortal
Knows not why change attracts him so,
Yet proves ever elusive.

No external force exists
To contradict centripetal force of cyclical life,
So life's mosaic perpetuates,
So no one square becomes misplaced.
Be changeless, life, though each life yearns
To excel the other, yet knows not why,
Except to defy a tested pattern.

Be gone, each grain of life,
Insignificant as each other, each clinging
To the wind; the same pre
And post existing. For from birth
Each soul is dying; time shall
Pass, yet soul remains unchanging.
Every grain is every other.
No change ever befalls
Life's silenus.

Vanessa Jackson (16)
Ballymena Academy

The Changing Wind

Old trees are creaking and swaying,
Leaves are falling in multitudes.
Like snowflakes they cover the ground.
Grass is moving this way and that.
Urged on by the ever changing wind.

The sea is so angry and grey,
It crashes into the high cliffs.
The waves are like mighty stallions,
Tossing foam far into the sky.
Urged on by the ever changing wind.

Bright clothes on the line are twisting,
Drying as soon as they are hung.
People bent double like beggars,
Are scurrying quickly along.
Urged on by the ever changing wind.

Rachael Mckillen (11)
Ballymena Academy

Friendship Lost

How long should I mourn
For our friendship lost?
It was if it was scorned,
Did we know the cost?
Those long conversations,
Those joyful walks.
A person to lean on,
When the others mocked.
We got a feeling of peace,
Every time you were near.
Never a sad face,
One thing we held dear.
But now it's gone,
Like rubbish tossed.
How long should I mourn
For our friendship lost?

Samuel Steele (13)
Ballymena Academy

Everywhere

Have you ever felt the sun
On a frozen winter's day?
Have you ever felt expressive
But had nothing new to say?
Have you ever felt the world is against you
And been surrounded by your friends?
Have you ever wanted a new beginning
Before the last one even ends?
Have you ever felt alive
But deep inside you are dead?
Have you ever felt fearless
While your mind fills up with dread?
Have you ever felt so happy
Because you have no more tears to cry?
Have you ever told the complete truth
For it to come out as a lie?
Have you ever loved someone so much
You just want to see the smile?
Have you ever felt rejected
When wearing a frown is the latest style?
Have you ever needed to talk
But been unable to open up?
Have you ever wanted something so much
But not been sure you are enough?
Cos baby, you know that's how I feel
Every time we touch.

Francesca O'Kane (14)
Ballymena Academy

I Wander . . .

Do they wander?
I wander.
I wander.
Slipping to other minds, other places.
My imagination holds no boundaries, no fencing.
My questions however lie unanswered,
In the deep crevices of my mind,
Away from my eyes,
Like doors ajar.
For them to see,
For them to know of my questions . . .
I could not bear.

I must be careful for maybe,
One day, in one moment,
My mind will wander,
Wander so far,
That it may not find its way back again.

Maybe, may it be possible,
For there to be others like me?
That wander?
Do you wander?

Jessica McAllister (12)
Ballymena Academy

The Enemy Call

I hear a noise,
A bleeping noise,
It's very far away,
Nothing much at all.
It's getting louder now,
Much more persistent;
I don't want it
Invading my dreams.
I'm beginning to recognise it,
It's the enemy,
It went away for two whole months,
But promised to return.
It has . . . it's here,
It's September - oh dear!

I open my eyes to face it,
It seems as if it grins.
I'm in control now;
The days, the hours, the minutes it bleeps
Surrender now to me.
I try to break free
But a black forbidding figure
Stands between me and the door.
I silence the enemy,
I had no choice,
I couldn't think with the noise.
Then I see it,
I surrender to the enemy call,
The black forbidding figure or rather
A new black uniform on the back of the door,
It's September - oh dear!

Jack Neeson (11)
Ballymena Academy

Growing Up

Days are hard when all you can do is lie still,
The whole world sits up but I can't,
My big brother sits up straight,
I wish I could do the same.

Days are hard when all you can do is sit up,
The whole world moves but I can't,
My big brother crawls around,
I wish I could do the same.

Days are hard when all you can do is crawl,
The whole world stands but I can't,
My big brother stands up tall,
I wish I could do the same.

Days are hard when all you can do is stand,
The whole world walks but I can't,
My big brother can walk so well,
I wish I could do the same.

Days are hard when all you can do is walk,
The whole world runs but I can't,
My big brother can run so fast,
I wish I could do the same.

Hooray, hooray,
I can stand and run and play,
My mum said I could do it one day
And she was right.

Days are hard when all you can do is run,
The whole world jumps but I can't,
My big brother can hop on one foot,
I wish I could do the same.

Hannah Douglas (13)
Ballymena Academy

A Rugby Match

I am mentally focused and ready to play,
the whistle blows and the ball is away.

The game has started, the crowd goes wild,
the adrenaline pumps and I'm excited inside.

I don't have the ball so what shall I do?
I shall tackle and ruck
'Til I'm covered in muck.

I have the ball, so what shall I do?
I shall run with the ball,
Then pass it to you.

I have the ball, so what shall I do?
I shall kick the ball
Or chip it through.

I have the ball, so what shall I do?
I shall side-step and drive
And score a try.

The game is over, the crowd goes wild,
We have won a trophy and are filled with pride.

Jonathan Holmes (12)
Ballymena Academy

Five Years Old

A five-year-old
eager to discover the world
hangs his head over the door
waiting for food and company.
He sees something move,
he starts niggling,
he doesn't stop until he gets what he wants!

A five-year-old
eager to discover the world,
is spooked by the silliest things:
a bag blowing in the wind,
a jumper with holes in it,
a plank with writing on it.
It will be a while yet!

A five-year-old
eager to discover the world
is the best friend I know.
He doesn't have to be human,
he listens to what I have to say,
he always has a shoulder I can cry on,
he will never let me down!

A five-year-old
eager to discover the world,
trusts me in every way,
he relies on me for everything.
Rain, hail, sleet or snow,
I have to be there.
Who else would care enough about him?

Louise Clarke (13)
Ballymena Academy

Beach Ride

His wild mane,
His flowing tail,
His gathered haunches
And pounding hooves
Make me feel free.

The morning sun
Is bright and cheery
As we gallop across
Soft, sandy beaches,
Just as one.

Slowing to a walk,
He snorts
And with a piercing whinny
He dances on the spot,
Fighting for his mouth;
I struggle for control,
My heart racing with excitement.

His eyes are rolling,
His coat foam-flecked.
The cold wind
Whips my face,
As both in high spirits,
Our beach ride ends.

Joann Andrews (13)
Ballymena Academy

I Am Happiest When . . .

I am happiest when I have begun a game,
    We win the ball,
    My opposition is small,
    I'm screaming and shouting,
    My teammates think I'm insane,
    We spread it out wide,
    I'm involved in a drive,
    I'm on a large pitch,
    The ball comes to me,
    I make a tremendous break,
    Their coaches shout, 'Watch his side-step'
    We take the lead,
    I make them concede,
    I begin to run wild and free,
    I sprint towards the line,
    I make them look feeble,
    I trick about ten,
    We score again,
    My kick soars over,
    My coach says, 'Same next week, men!'
    I reach home and rest
    (And start to wish again!)

Ricky Andrew (13)
Ballymena Academy

War

Why all this dying?
Why all this pain?
Why all this lying?
There's nothing to gain.

Why all this blame?
Why all this deceit?
Why all this grieving?
In a world full of shame.

Sirene Watt (13)
Ballymena Academy

The Safari Park

A fearsome growl,
An echoing roar,
A frightening sound
Beyond the gate.

A flash of gold,
A stripe of brown,
A whole pride
On the ground.

A pride of lions
Just next to me,
A leopard darts
Behind a tree.

A cheetah is racing
Towards its prey,
A lynx is waiting,
But we can't stay.

The sun is setting
And we must leave,
I say goodbye to
The magnificent game.

Alexandria Stewart (13)
Ballymena Academy

Chocolate

Dark, smooth, rich and creamy,
Solid, flaky, white and dreamy.
Filled with flowing caramel
Or in a sugar-coated shell.

How I love the matchless smell,
No need to look, as I can tell
The type of it, dark or light,
Milky, Belgian, snowy white.

Named after everything in space,
Each one is unique in taste.
There's Galaxy, Mars and Milky Way,
All of these I'd eat all day!

I'm chocolate, chocolate, chocolate mad,
I eat when happy and when sad.
I savour each and every bite,
Chocolate brings me such delight!

Kathy Michael (13)
Ballymena Academy

The Rush

There's a rush to get in and out of places
People want to get here, there and everywhere
Quickly,
Like a herd of oxen,
Everyone wants to be first in the dinner queue,
So they run,
Everyone pushes, shoves, barges,
Nobody wants to be last,
The force of the crowd is so strong,
Enough to bring a door crashing down,
Everyone has to be so violent,
It's just . . .
Complete . . .
Chaos!

Claire Hayes (12)
Ballymena Academy

The Movement Of The Feline And The Mouse

The feline is the predator, the mouse is the prey,
On this eventful harvest day.

The feline stalks the little mouse,
Who is far from his house.

Then something the mouse does hear,
He knows that a feline is near.

The mouse feels small and not so big,
The mouse is sweating like a pig.

The feline creeps up more and more,
The mouse doesn't know what's in store.

Just then the feline pounces,
Suddenly the little mouse bounces.

But the mouse is far too late
And he has a dinner date.

Grace Alexander (12)
Ballymena Academy

Movement

Still and tranquil, nervously awaiting
the flicker of the dawning of the day,
the jungle stirs and whispers
with every gentle move.

The baby monkey lovingly snuggles up,
its mother's arms caressing, her eyes wandering,
awaiting danger.
The snake wriggles through the long, flowing grass,
while the tiger stretches, turns his head looking around,
waiting.

The flytrapper strikes for its prey,
like a cat pounces on its prey.
A crocodile bites like a bear trap,
movement is all around us.

Camille Delpy (11)
Ballymena Academy

The Body Dance

We all love to move around,
Some without any sound,
Up and down, left and right,
Our muscles can get very right.
We bend and stretch,
To loosen up,
Arms and legs as heavy as lead,
Like when you just get out of bed.
Walking along, lifting my feet,
Wanting to make a dance to a groovy beat,
My head and shoulders are waiting their turn,
Fingers and toes humming along,
My whole body wants to swirl to the song,
Even my elbows are joining in,
Along with my shins and knees,
I now feel as if my whole body is on fire,
I can tell I'm beginning to tire,
My body is slithering down.

Andrina Elliott (11)
Ballymena Academy

Movement

The swerving of the players
Around each other,
Dribbling up the pitch
With lightning speed,
The swift movements
Of all the players,
The strikers dodging
All of the other team
And then the fierce strike
Of the ball into the net.

Glenn Kennedy (11)
Ballymena Academy

What's The Rush?

One day I looked around at a busy street,
People hurrying because of targets to meet,
At my house people also hurry,
'Why?' I said
'What's the flurry?'
Someone once said life's like a race,
The quicker you run, the faster the pace.
But I don't believe it,
It can't be true,
If life's like a race, what can we do?
Well I'm glad the only race I have to run
Is not for a ball,
It's at lunchtime,
To the dinner hall.

Naomi Lamont (13)
Ballymena Academy

A Windy Autumn Day

The trees are swaying
The children are playing
The wind is whistling
The leaves are fistling
The kites are flying
The leaves are dying
It's a windy autumn day

Autumn is here
The harvest is near
The power lines are humming
A storm is coming
The rain is pouring
The fire's roaring
It's a windy autumn day.

Sarah Lamont (11)
Ballymena Academy

Movement

Swirling lights that dazzle eyes,
Blending colours tempting shoppers.
Jostling bargain hunters spending eagerly.
Revolving doors that ferry people,
Ascending escalators climbing forever.
Wafting smells tantalising taste buds,
Trundling trolleys carry the weekly shop.
Plodding guide dogs faithfully lead,
Curling steam from rain-wet bodies.
Pawing dogs in pet shop windows,
Ambling pensioners chatting to friends,
Cuddling couples in a world of their own.
Dancing bears on display,
Bumping baby buggies to avoid,
Crawling queues for Hallowe'en toys,
Clambering children rushing for rides.
Sauntering security men: eyes peeled for trouble,
Gung-ho gangs roaming through crowds,
Descending elevators carry spent-out mothers,
Frenetic movement in the shopping centre!

James Burrows (12)
Ballymena Academy

Shadows

Walking along,
Another person beside me,
She's black,
Her name is Shadow.

Riding along,
Another horse beside me,
It's black,
Its name is Shadow.

Judith Thompson (12)
Ballymena Academy

The Chase

A flick of a tail as black as coal,
The high-pitched squeak of a mouse,
In the garden the cat chases its prey,
But the mouse escapes to the house.
The cat, he followed with intense speed,
As the mouse looks for his hole
Through the house the chase continues,
Dashing this way and that.
Who will win the marathon run,
The mouse or the big black cat?
The mouse is ahead, but just by a tail
And the cat is catching up fast
A woman screams as she sees the pair,
Quickly running past.
Suddenly the chase it ends, all in a black and grey blur,
The mouse is dead and the cat is happy,
And he breathes a contented purr.

Fiona Gibson (11)
Ballymena Academy

The Waltz

Together they glide out onto the stage,
Then in their twos, they all engage.
When they are ready, the stage starts to light,
Showing off their costumes so dazzling and bright.

The dance commences in steps of three,
Like walking down the street, they dance with ease.
This way, that way, striding along,
All of their movements like rounds in a song.

Then as the dance draws to an end,
They assemble politely, each one a friend.
Graciously they bow as the curtain falls
And applause overflows from the balcony and stalls.

Kirstie McKay (11)
Ballymena Academy

All About Me!
(Based on 'The Writer Of This Poem' by Roger McGough)

The writer of this poem is
As cheeky as a monkey,
As cool as a cat
And as lazy as a donkey.

As strong as a rock,
As happy as the sun,
As silly as a clown
And as sweet as a bun.

As nice as an apple,
As daft as a dog,
As nutty as a professor
And as stiff as a log.

As slow as a tortoise,
As kind as can be,
She's the best of them all
And yes it is me!

Deborah Millar (11)
Ballymena Academy

Unhappiness And False Smiles

A little jar beside my bed
So many secrets that it holds
All filled with tears that I have shed
A jar of memories to be told.
A time of pain and broken promises
Unfinished dreams and sacrificed happiness
Bruised mind and empty heart
Split in the middle and ripped apart
I'm building up the tears
Filling it to the top
Every time I'm thinking about you
I just don't know when to stop.

Stephanie Li (15)
Ballymena Academy

A Journey By Boat

Weather forecast warning,
Gale force winds and rain.
Ferries cancelled one by one,
But we were instructed to drive onboard.

Strong winds blew as we left the port,
Rain beat like drums on the windowpanes.
Waves crashed hard against the sides
And those on deck were soaked to the skin.

Crash, bang, was all we heard,
As the bottles tumbled off the shelves.
Bumping up and down, swaying side to side,
This journey was like a white-knuckle ride.

Children crying, adults pale with fright,
As we looked around, what a sight!
It was much too late to change our minds,
We'd started so we'd have to finish.

At last the coast was within our sight,
This journey like a nightmare, was almost over.
Sighs of relief were heard by all,
As the boat finally docked at the harbour.

Amy Stewart (11)
Ballymena Academy

Sitting In Silence

Sitting in this traffic jam
For at least half an hour,
Getting so bored of the
Stillness of this car,
Why aren't we moving?
This is starting to annoy me,
I really want to know,
I'll die of curiosity,
Same old songs on the radio,
I'm angry now, it's starting to show,
Lack of movement,
What's holding me back?
I'm going to be late,
I'm starting to crack,
Starting to move but we're
Going quite slow,
I can't see the problem
But we are getting ready to go,
Letting out rage,
Yet starting to drive,
What's up with this time
Of which I've been deprived,
When I can see,
My heart slowly sinks,
I've been so selfish,
It's an accident, 3 cars
Smashed, 4 lives trashed.

Christine Rock (11)
Ballymena Academy

Donegal

In the far north west of Ireland
Lies a place that is well known,
Hills and valleys, shimmering seas
Friendly folk in every town.

We know it now as Donegal
But I like the name from the past,
Tirconnel was what it used to be
And that name will surely last.

I have a brother living there
In a place close by the sea,
Whins and brambles all around
And a burn flows quietly.

I love to go to that great place
To see Rowan and Anne-Marie
And play games with Jordan and wee Adam
And paddle in the sea.

Time spent in lovely Donegal
Or Tirconnel, if you prefer,
Is something to look forward to
I'm glad I'm often there.

Rebecca Hall (11)
Cambridge House Grammar School

The Snake

Well, for a start,
The snake hasn't got any heart.
Snapping and cracking across the jungle floor,
Slithering up to the old wild boar.
Pounce!
But the old snake doesn't get an ounce,
The wild boar roams free
And the snake has to get another ticket fee!

Diane Montgomery (12)
Cambridge House Grammar School

My Room

A medium sized room;
With a brown door.
Inside the room;
Lovely bright sky-blue walls;
With a little silver.
Two large windows
At either side
And long blue and silver curtains,
As you walk through the door;
There are three small wardrobes
Unusual bunk beds too.
To the right you'll see;
Four small drawers;
Packed with school books.
On top of the drawers;
A TV and video player
And high up on the wall;
Is a stereo player;
So that no little hands;
Can touch it,
Because that's my room.

Stephanie Dowds (13)
Cambridge House Grammar School

School

I get up early in the morning
To make my way to school,
I feel so tired sitting on the bus,
I feel like such a fool,
Tonight for sure I'll go early to bed,
So in the morning I'll be bright in the head,
Then when I meet my friends at school,
I'm no longer tired, I'm just cool!

Lauren Ferguson (11)
Cambridge House Grammar School

The Greatest Match

The footballers step onto the pitch
Most of them are very rich
It's Manchester United Vs Real Madrid
The referee is Neil Ratrid

They line up to sing the national song
They've been waiting for this match all day long
And so the starting whistle goes
The fans are seated in the rows

It's Scholes to Ronaldo, oh what a pair
Not like Beckham and his girlie hair
And Nistelrooy opens the scoring
The fans are ecstatic and they're roaring

Come on United, only ten minutes to go!
The Madrid fans are keeping low
It's 1-0 and the end of the match
Man United will be hard to catch.

Jamie Craig (11)
Cambridge House Grammar School

Hallowe'en

H allowe'en is a time of fun
A t dark the children come out to play
L ike lightning fireworks go up
L aughter and joy of families having fun
O ld people trying to sleep
W ild bonfires burning like crazy
E ating toffee apples and candy
E njoying the great fun
N oises of dogs in the dark night.

Kathryn McWhirter (11)
Cambridge House Grammar School

My Trouble Secret Pet

He tore up the carpet,
Mum thought it was me,
He scored the table,
Mum thought it was me.

He chewed all the wires,
Mum thought it was me.
He smashed Mum's glasses,
Mum thought it was me.

He ripped up Mum's paperwork,
Mum thought it was me,
He dented Mum's car,
Mum thought it was me.

Because I'm on my own at home,
Mum blames it all on me.
When things go wrong around the house,
Mum blames it all on me.

I told my mum about my friend,
She says she understands,
She didn't know about my friend,
But now she understands.

I introduced her to my friend,
She thinks he's really nice,
When things go wrong around the house,
It's not always down to me.

Claire McIntosh (12)
Cambridge House Grammar School

Blind Life

Blind life is miserable,
Everything's invisible.
Life is lonely and sad,
But when a friend's around
And you feel down,
Count on them to make you glad.

When you're out and about with a walking stick
And glasses black as coal,
Everyone stops and stares
And you're without a know.

Whenever you get home and pray to God,
'What did I do wrong?'
Always remember, you're number one
And bring a friend along.

You can always count on a friend
When they're about
Because that's what friends are for,
Whatever the person, they should help,
Whenever you begin to cry,
Because that's what friends are for.

Trevor Shiels (11)
Cambridge House Grammar School

Sport

I like sport,
The running around, all over the ground,
Hitting the ball, scoring for all,
The cheers of the crowd, make me feel proud,
We jump up and scream, we're the best team.
We're one-nil up, we want the cup,
We roar like a bear, we're nearly there,
That's it done, we have won,
We're going out the gate, to celebrate!
I like sport.

Neil Davidson (12)
Cambridge House Grammar School

Where Is The Place?

I love it!
It's sunshine-yellow,
With a hint of red,
Where is the place that's mine?

Cosy,
I chill out here,
All the time,
I see objects around,
But where is the place that's mine?

There are art pencils,
Violin with a stand,
Window with a view,
But where is the place that's mine?

Of course!
Didn't you know?
It's my bedroom,
I love it, it's mine.

Emma Smith (13)
Cambridge House Grammar School

Why?

Pink and blue is all you see,
The room could have been done more colourfully,
Beds, one big, one small,
I wish I had a bedroom like the hall.

Sheets on the bed are a blue, blue, blue,
With little bits of hard nail glue.
It's so tall, it's hard to climb,
Why can't I have a bedroom that doesn't look like mine.

I can't understand,
How Mum likes it,
It's horrible, horrible,
Please give me a new bedroom.

Mollie Arthur (13)
Cambridge House Grammar School

The Bright Blue Hue

The bright blue hue,
Jumping out of the wall,
Pity about the untidiness though.
A never-ending pile of clothes, a skateboard that injures every visitor,
Music *booming* out of an un-coordinating yellow radio.

In the half open wardrobe, lies a jungle of junk jumbled together,
Old toys, oversized hand-me-downs, stained glass bottles.
Only one desk 'dedicated' to tidiness.
A gleaming mirror sits on the desk,
Half-filled tubs, lined up like soldiers saluting.

The curtains are drawn slightly,
Revealing a thin line of light and a few houses in the distance,
The bin is overflowing with sweet wrappers, Coke cans and
                                                crisp packets.

A dark green uniform lies scattered on the floor,
On the bed lies a little blue bunny with one eye gazing out,
One slipper sits on the floor,
The other one? Well, I'll get it later.

Oh well, time to tidy up again,
There's no point, I mean, it'll be just the same tomorrow,
But it's nice this way,
The bright blue hue.

Jenny Bradley (12)
Cambridge House Grammar School

Winter Wind

A cold wind blows across the snowy street,
Children run and play, throwing round snowballs,
On the large frozen lake everyone falls.
Everyone wanders around with frozen feet,
People are cold and need to burn some peat,
To keep nice and warm in their cosy halls,
Cold shop owners shivering at their stalls,
Selling their wares under a frozen sheet.
A robin sits on the near window sill,
The other birds look for feed from the tree,
So through the winter they will get their fill.
Christmas is coming so time for a tree,
Sending good wishes and lots of goodwill,
It is the most exciting time for me.

Steven Cooper (15)
Cambridge House Grammar School

Winter's Park

A freezing cool breeze hits my rough, red face
Soft, flaky snow falls gently on the ground
Many cold hard seats lay bare, make no sound
I see the rusty, broken swings in place
A revolting rat runs past at quick pace
Everywhere is dark, nothing to be found
Just a loud barking dog acts like a hound
The sky darkens slowly as I tie my lace
I get up slowly, frozen by the frost
Walk slowly to the gate feeling lost
I open the tall dark gate with no key
Not an animal or person I see
Nearer I get to my home for my tea
The snow falls rapidly, sparkling on me.

Steven Herbison (14)
Cambridge House Grammar School

The Match

The sound of cheering broken out in the crowd
Our team had just scored a wonderful goal
He celebrated by doing a roll
I never heard the stadium so loud

The other team scored to make it square
I was in shock with my hands on my head
All I could think of *relegation*, dread
So I sat down quietly on my chair

There were a few chances for us to score
But the other team's defence was too strong

I just thought to myself no more, no more
I lost faith in my team how wrong, it's wrong

I knew my team would have something in store
So we all stood up and started our song.

Mark Robinson (14)
Cambridge House Grammar School

Portrush Sonnet

A lovely blue sky and not a cloud in sight,
The twinkling sound of the ice cream van,
Playful drawings surround the plump jolly man,
Hungry seagulls are in their full flight,
They are flapping their wings with all their might,
Sandy golden beaches are filled with people,
See the outline of the church steeple,
Sun glittering on the sea so bright,
I went to Barry's, the amusement park,
I took a car alone on the ghost train,
Scary monsters popped out of the eerie dark,
Waiting for me outside was my friend, Jayne,
We love Barry's, we always have a lark,
I took a picture and put it in a frame.

Jill Surgenor (14)
Cambridge House Grammar School

Hallowe'en

It's the favourite time of year for me
Hallowe'en brings joy and glee
Thinking of it makes me tingle
Like it's something really special

Witches with cats and long pointy hats
Flying in the sky are bats with rats
Owls hooting in the trees
Is something that scares me

As fireworks go into the sky
I watch them with a close eye
The Catherine wheels and rockets
Both hands deep in my pockets

Hallowe'en will soon be over
I'll have to wait 'til next October
I shouldn't look so blue
'Cause there's Christmas to look forward to.

Kathryn Watt (11)
Cambridge House Grammar School

Sense-ational

Burgundy berries, round and juicy
Tempt my bursting taste buds.
Amber, russet, chestnut and ochre
Create a carpet of colour.
Bonfire smoke, popcorn and apples melt into the mingling mist
Crusty, wrinkly, crinkly leaves
Are crushed beneath my feet.
Birds chatter, squawk and squabble
As they forage for a harvest feast.
Full and plump, luscious and juicy
This truly is a sense-ational time.

Ellen McCartney (11)
Cambridge House Grammar School

My Perfect Black Rose

My perfect rose has petals, dark as night,
Surrounded in clouds of misty despair.
No lost soul have I ever seen so fair,
Its petals shine to give an eerie light,
A guidance to souls losing will to fight.
In death's own touch do we find its dark lair,
A symbol of a long forsaken prayer.
My thorny, perfect black rose shining bright,
Oh why do people fear my perfect rose?
Its mystery tells a truth forgotten,
Alas, my perfect black rose stands to lose,
Purpose in a world, sinfully rotten.
It's losing the battle against its foes,
My perfect black rose is gone, forgotten.

Laura Bowman (15)
Cambridge House Grammar School

I Hate School

I hate school
The scratch of pens on paper,
The clicking of the stapler,
The bustle of students walking,
The boom of people talking,
The banging of the doors,
The number of different floors,
The reading of the books,
The very sleepy looks,
I hate school.

Sabrina Rodgers (11)
Cambridge House Grammar School

Rugby Fan

The Twickenham arena, made me small,
Grayson kicked a drop-kick over the posts,
That made the lead bigger over the hosts,
The team moved towards the line by a maul,
They made the lead bigger, over the hosts now,
He blew the whistle for the end of play,
The players ran on and the crowd cheered 'Yay!'
The crowd started to cheer, 'How! How! How!'
The play started with the kick of the ball,
The other team caught it and made a maul,
They collapsed the maul and scored a try,
I thought to myself, *this shirt I need to buy,*
The referee blew, we gave a great roar,
We couldn't believe the final score.

Aaron Osmer (14)
Cambridge House Grammar School

Shadows

I have a shadow that always seems to be with me
And what's the use of it is more than I can see
It's really very like me from my feet to my head
And I see him beside me when I go to bed

The funny thing about him is the way he likes to grow
Not at all like me or you, which is very slow
For he sometimes shoots up tall like a bouncy ball
And he sometimes gets so small there's no sign of him at all

He hasn't got a notion of how children should play
And he always makes a fool of me in every kind of way
He stays so close beside me, he's a coward you can see
I'd feel awful to stick to Mummy as that shadow sticks to me.

Diana Smyth (14)
Cambridge House Grammar School

I Like Sport

I like sport
The cries of the fans and supporters
The players' hearts run like motors
The tries and the goals and
The scorer, Michael Mols
The defence, the midfielders and the strikers too
The objective is to stick to your opponents like glue
The keeper who keeps on making saves
The fans and supporters do Mexican waves
The full time approaches
The worried faces on the coaches
The players getting tackles in
The teams really want to win
The whistle starts to ring
The fans start to sing
I like sport.

Darren Rodgers (12)
Cambridge House Grammar School

Midnight Ocean

As I stand here in the sand
I feel the water
Trickling around my toes
The smell of salt
In the cold midnight air
Pebbles washed up
On the shore
Smooth and round like never before
I wish I could stay here in the sand
Forever and ever and evermore.

Emma Magowan (13)
Cambridge House Grammar School

Football Sonnet

The grass was green with white lines around it
The stadium was brilliant and so tall
Compared to it the players looked so small
To see the match you had to stand, not sit
The crowd were singing bit by bit
The crowd all around was like a big wall
Sometimes it was hard to see the football
The stadium was like a massive pit
Giggs ran down the wing taking on Ashley Cole
He tricked him with a good feint, what a con
Crossed it in for Fletcher to score a goal
Nearly all of the Arsenal fans were gone
For a celebration he did a roll
Scholes jumped on Fletcher and the rest piled on.

Lee Megaw (14)
Cambridge House Grammar School

Ballymena Town

The summer is over, days were long
But suddenly autumn and winter dawn
The days are shorter, get dark at six
Heavy long clothes, we are in a fix
The temperatures are falling
The frost, not far away
I know it's only starting
But I long for summer's day
We'll have Hallowe'en and fireworks
There'll be apples, nuts and all
And if we're lucky perhaps a Hallowe'en ball
The next thing will be Christmas
When the snow is on the ground
That's what's going to happen in Ballymena Town.

Karen McQuillan (15)
Cambridge House Grammar School

Animals

I like animals
The bleat of sheep in grassy fields
The yelp of a dog that never heels
The grunt of pigs lazing in their sties
The chirping of birds flying in skies
The buzzing of bees humming at flowers
The squeal of rats gnawing for hours
The cawing of crows in farmers' fields
The hiss of snakes whose skin they yield
The hoot of owls all through the night
The howl of wolves that give you a fright
The mooing of cows all night in the barn
The quack of ducks around the farm
I like animals.

Gary Worthington (11)
Cambridge House Grammar School

The New York Subway Scene

Standing staring at the wall in the dim,
Dirty water in a puddle on the floor,
A place I go each day that's such a bore,
The rats on the platform scraping the bin,
The homeless lying seems a sin,
Lying in the archway of the lift door,
Their arching bodies must be really sore,
Surviving on only a bottle of gin,
Their home a lot of years is so damp,
To get on the train there's such a big shove,
'Mind the gap' and 'There's a broken-down ramp',
Warming their hands on a fire and gloves,
The homeless again sitting in their camps,
They need some more peace, a sign of a dove.

Lynsey McNeilly (14)
Cambridge House Grammar School

I Hate Cruelty

I hate cruelty,
Big men with tiny cages,
Putting big animals in there for ages,
'Dogs Trust' now that's a good place,
Plus, there is a lot of space,
People think animals don't matter,
But that's not true,
Because they do,
People put animals in a zoo,
Zoos let endangered animals stop dying out,
Yet some circuses are good because
They let animals get out and about,
What have the poor animals ever done to you?
Nothing! So stop hurting them and give them respect, please do,
I hate cruelty.

Jenna Fleck (11)
Cambridge House Grammar School

I Like Cars

I like cars
The rev of an engine
The toot of a horn
The screech of the tyres which are warming at dawn
The puff of an exhaust which is damp and clouded
The splash of the wipers on a rainy day
The plop of the rain on the newly painted roof
The boom of a crash which explodes through the air
The echo of death is distant and rare
The only thing that brings joy to my ears
I like cars.

David Boyd (12)
Cambridge House Grammar School

I Like Horses

I like horses
The thud of a hoof, the crunch by a tooth
The twitch by an ear, I wish I could hear
The swish of a tail, it never shall fail
The sweet smell of hay makes my pony neigh
She runs through the fields and has such fun
She chases others through fields of straw
The cows all moo as she runs by
She jumps over brightly coloured walls
And wins many rosettes for me
I love her so much, she's my honeybee
I like horses.

Julie McCrory (11)
Cambridge House Grammar School

Sport

I like sport
The crackle of a gun, the joy of a run,
The roughness of rugby, it can turn ugly,
The game football is played with a round ball,
The excitement of baseball, try and catch the ball,
The gush of wind when I run,
The high jump, it's different from the long jump,
The speed of a car, that's won by far,
The silence of fishing, the water swhishing,
The long walks in golf must be good for your health,
The fifteen balls in pool are two colours as a rule,
I like sport.

Josh Rea (12)
Cambridge House Grammar School

Home

'Home is where the heart is'
Or so they say
My heart is in the country
That's where I live today

Home is where you lay your head
After a tiring day
When it is time to go to bed
To rest and sleep before the fray

Home is the smell of fresh baked bread
To satisfy my hunger
Gather round ready to be fed
When you just can't wait any longer

Home is where I feel warm
Loved as one of the family
Away from danger and harm
I feel my home
Homely.

William Davidson (13)
Cambridge House Grammar School

I Like TV

I like TV
The laugh of a human, the squeak of the mouse,
The yelp of a cat, the bangs in the house,
The smile of the children, the bang of the gun,
The cry of a baby is so much fun,
The eyes of the mother watch over her child,
As they watch TV when the crowds go wild,
The laugh of the granny as she watches the street,
The coos of the baby when she tickles her feet,
We watch football and golf and all sports we enjoy,
But the peace is interrupted when Mum shouts, 'Lift that toy,'
I like TV.

Gary Bell (11)
Cambridge House Grammar School

I Hate School

I hate school
The waking up knowing you're going to school
When everyone round you is acting so cool
They'll give crocodile tears when homework's not done
Teachers forgive them, the pupil has won
I don't like the homework, too much I do think
And some of the teachers they really don't think
The chatting of girls, the fussing of boys
I really do wish there were lots of toys
There's too many steps and too many floors
When entering the classroom, knock on the door
I hate school.

Gemma Dornan (12)
Cambridge House Grammar School

I Like Minis

I like Minis
The broom of the car, the sound of the music,
The screech of the tyres rubbing on the ground,
The puff of the exhaust smoking away,
The crash of the car bouncing on the ground,
The scream of the people running from its grip,
The rumbling of the car coming down the stairs,
The whoosh of the car flying in the air,
The cry of the people who fainted in the dust,
The shouts of the people driving the car,
The rev of the car speeding away,
I like Minis.

Jonathan McKinney (11)
Cambridge House Grammar School

I Like Animals

I like animals
The miaow of a cat, the bark of a dog
The squeak of a mouse, the croak of a frog
The neigh of a horse, the moo of a cow
The cluck of a hen, the snort of a sow
The hoot of an owl, the hiss of a snake
The baa of a sheep, the bubbles from a hake
The stripes on a tiger, the roar of a lion
The cackle of a goose, the colour of a python
The fistle of a hamster, the ee-aw of a donkey
The spots from a giraffe, the bananas from a monkey
I like animals.

Emma McClintock (11)
Cambridge House Grammar School

I Like Sport

I like sport
The splash of water in my face
The gust of wind while I race
The way the ball blows away
The way we win on a sunny day
When every day I play cricket
I normally always hit the wicket
When I pass someone the ball
They nearly always seem to fall
I like sport.

Sara Kennedy (12)
Cambridge House Grammar School

I Like Irish Dancing

I like Irish dancing
The feeling when I jump up in the air
The pretty dresses that everyone wears
The way you are flying around the room
While someone plays in line to the tune
I like it when you can move to the beat
And also the way we dance with our feet
Making new friends for the rest of our lives
Knowing that Mum is watching with delight
Cheering us on to dance our very best
Happy to win medals or something else
I like Irish dancing.

Emily Hill (12)
Cambridge House Grammar School

Colours

I like colours
The red of roses, the blue of the sea
The yellow of the sun looking down on me
The green of the grass, the pink of the fairy
The white of the milk, fresh from the dairy
The purple of violets, the black of coal
The grey of a rainy day, very dull
The brown of chocolate, the orange of a fox
The gleam of a new toy, sitting in its box
The colours are pretty, they brighten my day
Use them well, don't lock them away
I like colours.

Jill Robinson (12)
Cambridge House Grammar School

Autumn Is Approaching

Autumn is approaching
Leaves will soon be falling
We will all be out raking them up
Then the next day it will be just as bad again

Hallowe'en will soon arrive
We will get a ring at our doorbell
Next we will hear the children screech, 'Trick or treat?'
They all look so nice and sweet
We will give them a fifty pence and a sweet each

Next it will be the cold dreary days of winter
The dark, cold mornings and evenings
When you need a coat and a hat
Then the snow begins to fall
Oh winter has its good points and bad points.

Lynsey Cathcart (13)
Cambridge House Grammar School

Return To Rathlin

The wind blew gently over the sea
And the clouds started to fade away
Rathlin is different from home
Belfast is busy and noisy but
Rathlin time stands still
An odd gull flies overhead
And a boat flies by
I thought I missed here
Maybe not.

Ricky Smyth (14)
Cambridge House Grammar School

Country Homes

Home is tall trees in the clouds,
Home is animals running around,
Home is tractors driving up and down,
Home is flowers in the ground.
Home is pink and yellow flowers,
Home is dew in the grass,
Home is birds flying above,
Home is leaves on the ground.
Home is family and friends,
People who you can depend on,
Home is cosy rooms and fires,
Home is cows in the byres,
Home is the best place in the world,
When you have family and friends.

Aaron Crawford (14)
Cambridge House Grammar School

City

You are holding your mum's hand
Then you run off to look at a toy shop
You look around and your mum's not in sight
You're all alone in the city

The buildings are tall all around
People are like giants
Uncaring and do not notice your cry
You're all alone in the city

Then out of the crowd of people
Your mum comes running with her arms open
You run and hug her
You're not alone in the big city!

Adam McCready (13)
Cambridge House Grammar School

Granny's Farm

I used to go to my granny's farm,
A compendium farmhouse,
Far up the lane.
Cows in the fields lowing,
Little lambs jumping, skipping.
Granda and I used to dander
Through the fields, shouting
At sheep, collecting sticks.
I remember the big bull,
With its shiny, nose ring.
The piglets when they were born,
All baby-pink and wriggly,
I jumped amongst them laughing and shouting,
Oh how I wanted to keep one!
My cousins were frightened of the piglets,
How silly they were.
I remember my first ride on the tractor,
My granda took me down the lane,
It was brilliant!
Then my granda passed away,
The farm was sold
And Granny moved to town,
So ended the tractor rides
And the lazy days playing with the animals.

Stacey McAuley (14)
Cambridge House Grammar School

The City

The city is big
The city is bad
The city is good
The city is rad

On one side we have
People doing good
Kind and loving
Doing all they should

On the other we have
People doing bad
Nasty and cruel
Everybody sad

We get good and bad
From the city but
We don't get mad
But sometimes sad

There are some things
In the city that
People have dreamed of
But it really is just
Chaos and disaster.

Peter Hughes (13)
Cambridge House Grammar School

Animals

I like animals,
The rrrroar of a lion, the grumpfles of a pig,
The schlurp of an anteater, the dogs' mumfling when they dig,
The mreeorr of a cat, the scuttles of a spider,
The squeals of a fruit bat, preparing to be a glider,
The trumpet of an elephant, the squeaks of a tiny mouse,
When he finds some food along the way of looking for a house,
The bzzzt of a bee, the padding of a fox,
The panting of a hamster, asleep in his box,
The clopping of a horse, the mooing of a cow,
The twittering of a bird, sitting on a bough,
I like animals.

Lorraine Frew (12)
Cambridge House Grammar School

Get To School, Son

Come on, come on, come on
It's time to get to school, Son
Hurry up it's time to go to school
Now I have to clean that Ribena pool

Get to school, Son
You're making a mess
Get to school, Son
You're giving me stress

It's time to go to school, Son
You have to go because I am your mum
Come on, Son, hurry up
Oh! Put down that spilt Ribena cup.

Michael Blair (11)
Cambridge House Grammar School

The Kick

I was standing in the silence
The wind was blowing in my face
The tension was mounting
And the game was tied
The clock was counting down
To the last minute of play
I lined myself up for the kick
And I took two steps forward
And kicked the ball sky-high
It seemed to float in the air
But it came down right between the posts
The crowds stood up and roared
I had won the game for my team.

Philip Houston (13)
Cambridge House Grammar School

Autumn Begins And Ends

Summer slips away,
Autumn creeps
Upon the waiting world.
Colouring leaves fall
In heaps,
On the frosty ground.
The baring trees sit still in the blowing wind,
The orange-brown, crispy leaves
Blow away in the sightless wind.
When the leaves leave the now-bared trees,
Autumn leaves,
Winter wakes.

Rachael Murphy (13)
Cambridge House Grammar School

Night

The twinkling of the stars
The skirt of red light
Fears all now banished in that indescribable peacefulness
Glints of light, weaving a pattern of light
The moon half-eclipsed by a wandering cloud
The undisturbed peacefulness, that priceless sensation of total calm
The moon three-quarters visible awakening from its day-long siesta
Two lines of cloud defile the moon
The trees form gnarly figures on the horizon
Lonely and forlorn in the midnight breeze
The faint wisps of textured cloud drifting aimlessly and sad
On the wind of the evening
The moon now with a textured, black line etching through it
Like a river through it
The hazy blackness fringed with blood dissolves all fear
                                              into wisps of mist
The sound of cold, gentle wind flowing through the trees
A perfect peace, a whole peace
Diffusing from the moon and stars
A lone dog barks in the distance shattering the silence
While the moon floats on a carpet of cloud,
Black and solid
Soft and gentle
The moon arises to its full majesty and glory
This is a perfect peace
This is my peace.

Timothy Wright (13)
Cambridge House Grammar School

The View

Looking through the glass I am greeted
By a sight of familiar things I know

Tall, mysterious trees hunch in the chilling wind
Screeching, frustrated as their peace is disturbed

The sky above looms, keeping watch
Waiting to send its next attack

And as it grows dark, all is silent
All is dead, until suddenly without warning

The wind lurches, swinging through the trees
The sky rumbles, cackling at the sight

Of buckets, clattering along the ground
Leaves being battered and torn from their snug nests

Chaos, panic, fear reflects in the graggy
Puddles, the steamy, dirty windows

And then, it's over, stopped, but not
For long, it never surrenders

The sun peeps through the clouds, cautious
Weary, but with danger out of sight

It pours its rays over the land
And once again peace is regained.

Kerry-Leigh Doran (14)
Cambridge House Grammar School

My Walk Home

I have to walk home today
And I hate it
It is too cold
Feeling the ice-cold wind
Hitting against my face
Sends shivers down my spine
Leaves are blowing everywhere
And I can hardly see
Where I am
Mist fills the sky
And as it falls
It puts droplets onto the
Leaves and grass
Seeing home
I know I am not far away
Even though I am probably just
Seeing things
The rain is getting harder
And a lot colder
My house really comes
Into sight
Finally
Just a few steps away
And I can already feel the warmth
At last, I am home
The warmth, being home
And being away from the rain,
Feels like . . .
Heaven!

Kaitlin Taylor (14)
Cambridge House Grammar School

A Winter's Day

The snow falls like pieces of paper
Flittering from side to side
All animals and creatures lie dormant
And trees bare without leaves
School's out
Let's celebrate
Children already out playing, making snowmen
Children throwing snowballs to each other
As if smoking cigarettes in the cold
And dressed up like marshmallows to keep out the cold
Sledges zoom by as if rockets on ice
Parents slipping and sliding on the sidewalk
Finding it hard to stay on their feet
Christmas has come
Let's all have fun
Yet children are fearing
School is only days away.

Christopher Rock (14)
Cambridge House Grammar School

Dolphin

A sea skimmer,
An ocean glimmer,
A shore sleeper,
A summer weeper,
A water dream,
A speeding beam,
A swimming star,
A super splasher by far,
A wonderful creature,
A beautiful beach feature.

Alicia Mason (12)
Cambridge House Grammar School

The Dentist

Sitting at home,
I'm thinking,
Today's that day,
The day of angst and hate,
That comes every six months.

Into the waiting room,
That dark, dismal waiting room,
The place of reckoning,
Shivering in my chair,
The dark man calls.

I'm next,
It's me,
Not now,
I don't want to go,
It's time.

Into the room I go,
Still quaking in my boots,
Over to the chair I go,
I shut my eyes,
Off goes the metallic whir of the drill.

Gary Pollock (14)
Cambridge House Grammar School

Tony Hawk

A skateboard that is starting to crack
A Porsche that's running out of petrol
A knife that's going blunt
A giant of extreme sports that's starting to shrink
A shining star that's starting to fade
A carpet that's starting to lose its colour
A diamond that has lost its sparkle
Chips that have gone cold!

Adam Uprichard (11)
Cambridge House Grammar School

You Have To Go To School

You have to go to school today
You're doing my head right in
If I don't make you go to school today
You'll climb right back in that bin

You have to go to school today
I'd rather have you there
I don't want you sitting in the window
As if you don't even care

You have to go to school today
Yes, yes you do
I don't want you hitting the skirting board
But alas, alas you do

You have to go to school today
You're acting like a fool
You can't go to the pool today
'Cause I'm taking you to school.

Shelley Malcolmson (11)
Cambridge House Grammar School

What Do I Know About Poems?

A poet laureate
I am not!

Tall and awkward
Is what I got!

Clever and shrewd
Would have been good!

Must find some way
To pay for my food!

Mum says!

Sophie-Smyth (12)
Cambridge House Grammar School

Cats And Dogs

I'm a dog not a cat,
So I've only got one
And I'm glad I've got one,
Unlike some who have none.

I'm walking round my house,
Not looking for a mouse.
Unlike them cats,
We got better stuff than that.

We will find their spies
And pop out their eyes,
Their resistance is futile,
Their cries will sound, *miaow*.

They have more lives,
But we have the spies.
Their lives will drop like flies,
But ours will match our size.

We've got guts, a courageous type,
All they've got's flab.
We lead a much more active life,
All they do is catnap.

We even look nicer,
All lovely and cute.
While all of them fat cats,
Deserve to go down the shoot.

They deserve to be locked up in cages,
Which is what we plan to do.
Then dogs will be the only pets,
To be loved and cared for by humans.

Ben Houston (12)
Cambridge House Grammar School

The Vamp

In the shadows,
Behind me,
There was the vamp,
Looking for Lee.

White as a ghost,
Black sleek hair,
Teeth as sharp as a knife,
She'd come out of her lair.

Like a bat in the air,
She flies over me,
Growing weaker by the minute,
Then she spots Lee.

She swoops down on his neck
And sucks on his blood,
Her batteries are charged,
Lee falls with a thud.

She takes off like a plane,
Because dawn is near breakin',
To get into her coffin,
Before the whole world is awakin'.

Anna-Margaret Moreland (11)
Cambridge House Grammar School

Cowboy

A six shooter
An Indian booter
A sly captor
A horse master
A land fighter
A strange talker
A funny walker
A village looter
An accurate shooter.

Steven Crawford (12)
Cambridge House Grammar School

My Arsenal Poem

Arsenal,
Arsenal,
Are the best,
Better than all the rest,
They always win, they never lose!

When Arsenal score a goal,
The crowd yell and cry for more,
Arsenal,
Arsenal
Oh, Arsenal we all adore!

When Campbell scores a goal, the crowd let out a roar,
Campbell,
Campbell,
You're our man,
Don't let us down if you can!

Arsenal,
Arsenal,
Are the best,
Better than all the rest,
They always win,
They never lose.

Oh, Arsenal you will be,
Always the team for me,
Because you always win,
You never lose!

Jordan Moore (11)
Cambridge House Grammar School

You Are Going To School, Son!

'Son, Son, won't you go away,
You've been rhyming in my ear for half the day,
You're going to school, no
You cannot stay,
Go away, oh go away.

Your truck will break,
The chairs will look old,
If you jump off the sofa, you're in for a scold,
You are going to school,
That is you told.

I don't care about shopping,
Or baking a cake,
You're going to school to give me a break.'

'Mummy, Mummy, please, no.'
'Go to school, Boy, go.'

Jordan Cumberland (11)
Cambridge House Grammar School

The Room

Room, room, room
A messy, messy room
Clothes lying everywhere
A car here and there
The train set's dusty
And an engine's really rusty
You can't even see the floor
And you can't open the door
Room, room, room
A messy, messy room.

Alastair Brunt (12)
Cambridge House Grammar School

The Flower

There was once an old ground patch
With nothing to be seen,
With not a thing covering it
Apart from the sun's beam.

The dry, crisp soil scattered all around,
Twirling and whirling close to the ground,
Then all of a sudden, the rain started planning
And out of the ground came a little green plantling.

It was days before it flowered,
But at last it came,
With the help from the sun
And the rain.

Now the grass is green beside a door,
The plant lives on as ever before,
Now you see the plant never dies,
The only thing this one plant is, is alive!

Victoria Lowry (11)
Cambridge House Grammar School

My Guinea Pig

A cabbage-eater
A squealing-rodent
A running-furball
A purring-bundle
A nose-licker
A toe-nibbler
A dark-hole-lover
An anything-eater
A towel-destroyer
A feet-warmer.

Rosalind Rowe (12)
Cambridge House Grammar School

My Sister

When we were young
We had some fun
Fighting and laughing at each other
And rolling about the ground

We did my mum's head in
She couldn't take it
If there was something really dear
We probably would break it

We thankfully now have grown up a bit
I like her now and she likes me too
I don't know what it would be like without her
She smells like my cat and snores like it too.

Amy Lester (12)
Cambridge House Grammar School

Autumn

The leaves are starting to spiral down
The colours are yellow, red and brown
Soon they start to carpet the ground
In the sky, not a swallow to be found

Hedgehogs gather in sleepy mood
Quite a large winter hoard of food
Snug and cosy in their set
Badgers fear not winter's threat

Frost sparkles as it lies on the tar
Dew freezes on the car
Night starts to eat away the day
Summer now has drifted away.

Jonathan Blaney (12)
Cambridge House Grammar School

I Want You To Go To School, Son

I want you to go to school, Son
I'll look after your duck
I want you to go to school, Son
The skirting board is tired of your truck
I'd rather you sit above the table
Leaving the varnish on the chairs

I want you to go to school, Son
Staying away from my feet
I don't want to go shopping with you, Steve
Just think about all of those bags that I would have to heave
I want to stop and talk to my friends, Son
Do you get that? Nice and clear?
I'd rather you sat down and learnt, Son
Shouting in no one's ear

Or how about a bit of learning?
I don't mind a bit of cutting out
As long as you do it in school, Son
Inside or out
What about a bit of maths, Son?
Two plus two is what?
I want you to come home with a big star, Son
Telling me about all of the things you have been taught

Your dad will be home later, Son
I shouldn't have given you that Ribena
Just look at that little pool
Do be quiet, Son, I am in a hurry
Oh, Son! Yes, Son, I am taking you to school.

Laura Brimley (11)
Cambridge House Grammar School

Orlando Bloom

He's an expensive oil painting
A sweet-smelling strawberry
A black silk shirt
A sharp sword
He's a mysterious adventure book
And a woman hunter
A burning candle in the wind
He's a long blond wig
A pair of black suede boots
A movie star
A treasure hunter
A pirate and blacksmith
He's a mysterious knight
And has dark locks.

Karen Munn (11)
Cambridge House Grammar School

Go To School Please, Son

I don't want you to stay at home, Son,
While you are getting under my feet,
You're not peeling the varnish off the chairs
And I'm not having you sitting on the stairs,
When you could be at school,
Rather than overflowing the sink and making a pool,
Remember the last time you tried to paint the dog's bone?
So leave the paint alone.
Son, don't put your legs out the window,
You could fall and break your elbow,
So get your bag and your coat,
Because guess what? You are going to school.

Rachel McBrinn (12)
Cambridge House Grammar School

Animals

Animals come in different sizes,
Thin, fat, small, tall,
Loads of animals get prizes,
Even if they're not the winner at all.

Loads of animals enter shows,
Sheep, horses, to and fro
And watch the dogs do their tricks,
When they won, they started to lick.

Animals are so much fun,
It does not matter who won,
In the end they're everywhere,
Land, sea and in the air.

Rachelle Lowry (12)
Cambridge House Grammar School

School

I want you to go to school, Daughter,
I can't have you at home today,
I've promised to go shopping,
With my younger sister, May.

I want you to go to school, Daughter,
Or you'll get under my feet,
I promise if you go to school,
I'll prepare a lovely treat.

Please go off to school, Daughter
And let your moaning cease,
'Cause when you are in school dear,
It gives my head some peace.

Philip Gordon (11)
Cambridge House Grammar School

My Dog, Ted

My dog is called Ted
And he lives in my bed,
He's brown with white spots
And he watches the clock,
He doesn't like strangers,
In case he's in danger,
When he sees a cat,
He'll bat it with his tail
And he always brings me my mail,
He's scared of the dark
And he likes a run in the park,
He likes his bones
And he eats them alone,
So don't go near Ted,
Or he'll eat your bones.

Jason Gault (11)
Cambridge House Grammar School

A Pen

A messy scribbler
A cruel writer
A funny typer
A weird drawer
An ink spiller
A kind poet
A smart brain
A word inventor
A special author
A different speller.

Amy Patterson (11)
Cambridge House Grammar School

I Want You To Go To School!

I want you to go to school, Son,
You're not staying home with your duck.
Get out from under the table, Love
And stop hitting my board with your truck.

I'm not leaving you on the stairs, Dear,
You'll be bored and - 'I don't care!'
Shh, please be quiet . . . hey - what's that noise?
Stop scratching the varnish off my chair!

I want you to go to school, Son,
I must get this washing hung out,
Put those scissors down, you'll cut yourself,
Do I always have to shout?

Here is that drink you asked for,
Now, what do you want to eat?
OK, pop your bum upon the drainer,
Put that down, you're not having that sweet!

Oh look, you've spilled her drink, Son,
Now, will you stop acting the fool?
Alright, that's it - I've had enough now,
Hurry up, grab your coat - we're going to school!

Alison Wright (12)
Cambridge House Grammar School

I Want You To Go To School, Son

I want you to go to school, Son,
Now hurry up, you'll have some fun,
Better than being at home all day,
You'll meet your friends and have time to play!

You'll do games and reading and then a break,
For milk and biscuits, then lunch to take,
From your Action Man lunchbox, oh what fun,
It's crisps and sandwiches and perhaps a bun!

Sarah Thompson (11)
Cambridge House Grammar School

I Want You To Go To School Today, Son

I want you to go to school today, Son
not stay at home with your duck
you'll not be staying at home with me, Son
so I wouldn't count on luck

I want you to go to school today, Son
not be underneath my feet
you're not coming shopping with me today, Son
in case of anyone we meet

You're not doing any painting today
not even any cutting out
you're not sitting out the open window
so don't give me that pout

Son, there's nothing at the bottom of the cupboard
nothing for you anyway
you're not jumping off the top of the sofa
why don't you just go to school and stay

Your dad is coming home soon, Son
that there is just some food
I don't know whose dog that is
and don't you be so rude

I'm taking you to school right now, Son
you've caused enough trouble for me
you're going to school right now, Son
before you send me crazy!

Laura Rankin (11)
Cambridge House Grammar School

Night Train

The night train runs along its tracks in the silent, starry night,
where the stars glitter and the moon's lit bright.
Passing through the countryside, passing trees whose shadows are
dark and long and the branches appear gangly and curled.
The train's windows glow dark red, with black outlines of tables and
seats appearing faintly through the mist and fog.
Every night, when the night train passes fields and rocky mountains,
the howl of the night wolf can be heard from the ghost town
                                        that lies ahead.
This town is where the train's station is. Silently and swiftly, the train
pulls up to the station.
The town around the station is deserted, except the ghost wolf,
who howls when the train has entered the town.
The buildings were destroyed by a war that had happened
                                        many years ago.
Apart from the ghost wolf and the night train, everything is dead but it's
the night train that leaves its tread.
But when the red morning sun rises, the night train fades away.

James McConnell (13)
Cambridge House Grammar School

Christmas

Christmas is coming,
The nights are getting chilly,
The leaves on the trees are falling,
The shops are crowded,
The streets are choc-a-block,
The shop windows are beautifully decorated
With toys and a Christmas tree,
The excitement that is building up,
To the fun of Christmas Day.

Simon Morton (13)
Cambridge House Grammar School

The Poodle

I have a pretty, pink poodle,
Her delightful name is Doodle.
Her hair is long and curly,
She is always in a hurry.

My friends call her Pom-Pom,
Others, Strawberry Bon-Bon.
She is my little girl
And has my world in a whirl!

Doodle always wears a pink bow,
It makes her eager eyes glow.
She has a pearly-pink lead,
Which is as clean as a bead.

In Doodle's little pink home,
You'll find her bed and grooming comb.
Her little pink bowl and drinking dish,
She enjoys chicken and fish.

Doodle has a fluorescent pink, cosy coat,
I don't want her getting soaked.
She is my furry, frizzy friend,
I will love her till the end.

Kathryn Young (14)
Cambridge House Grammar School

Storm Acrostic

S cared animals hurry to their homes to take cover.
T errified toddlers all snuggled up in their beds waiting
for morning to come.
O h how we love watching the storms at night.
R ain, pitter-patter on the windows and rooftops.
M ighty winds rattling against the windows.

Ricky Quigley (13)
Cambridge House Grammar School

If I Had Done My Homework Last Night

If I had done my homework last night
I wouldn't be here in detention.
If only I'd given a little more time
And paid a bit more attention.

I wouldn't be sitting writing 500 lines,
On the importance of doing my best.
If I'd just done my homework
And given the computer a rest.

Instead of being stuck in here, bored,
I could be out with my friends,
But when you're sitting in a deserted room,
The torment never ends.

If I had done my homework last night,
I wouldn't be here in detention.
If only I'd given a little more time
And paid a bit more attention.
(Have I said that before?)

Nikki Tweed (13)
Cambridge House Grammar School

Friends

I love you and you love me
And that's the way that friends should be.
We're sometimes happy, we're sometimes sad,
We're sometimes angry or even mad.

But I want you to know that I care for you,
This is true.
I love you and you love me
And that's the way that friends should be.

Hannah Carson (12)
Cambridge House Grammar School

My African Home

The only place to be
When you're as down as me,
The only bed that's safe and warm,
During an African thunderstorm.
The memories that filled my life with joy,
The place that I brought home my very first toy,
The place to hide from all my worries,
The walls could tell a thousand stories
And in my mind my memories roam,
It hurts so much to leave my home.
In shades of green, alone I stand,
Such beauty in this foreign land,
I won't despair 'cause I'll be back,
To live with my people both
'White' and 'black'.

Tristan Frame (13)
Cambridge House Grammar School

War

His long evil arms,
Grab you when you least expect it
Fingertips touching people's hearts
And bringing sadness to the world
His large feet stumping and sending
Vibrations through the Earth
His heart as cold as ice
And his heart sharp and painful
Hatred running through his veins
Like the hatred from the fighting countries!

Louise Cooper
Cambridge House Grammar School

The Sports Car

Quickly the car went,
Young and very rich,
Healthy as can be,
Beautiful and smooth,
Making a loud humming noise,
Echoing off the walls in the dark alley,
Parked on the side of the street,
Looking smart, handsome and proud,
Everybody staring at it,
As if it was a movie star,
It started up again,
Shooting out a gust of black smoke,
Making everyone choke
And skidded off again,
Roaming the streets like a king.

Jason Steele (14)
Cambridge House Grammar School

Magic

Magic can be pulling a rabbit from a hat,
Or turning a human into a bat.

Magic can make a python expand
And make a tortoise or turtle stand.

Magic can make lakes and rivers freeze
And turn tarantulas into bees.

With magic you could do almost anything you wish,
Even turn a saucepan into a dish.

Glenn McGivern (13)
Cambridge House Grammar School

I Wish . . .

I wish . . . I had a mansion way up in the hills,
            where my movie star husband
            would pay for all my bills.

I wish . . . in Spain I had a tan
            then every night I could
            visit my man.

I wish . . . I had a blue Mercedes
            just like Blu Cantrell
            and once I pick up Sean Paul,
            I'll be doing well.

I wish . . . I could stop daydreaming,
            because I keep getting told off in class,
            but I'm only in school for a couple more years,
            so I better make it last!

Deborah McCartney (14)
Cambridge House Grammar School

War

War has an evil smirk on his face
He forces the minds of two nations to fight.
He floats above the battlefield
His red horns shine
In the morning sun
He manipulates the minds of the soldiers to open fire
He laughs a high, horrific laugh
Flexing his muscles, he watches men die
His laugh dies away with the soldiers' lives
War is evil!

James Martin (14)
Cambridge House Grammar School

A Lonely Place

I'm screaming, but it's just an empty whisper.
I reach for a hand, but there's nobody to help me, again.
Shying away in a corner, speaking is too painful.
Eyes are watching, wondering, waiting in the shadows,
Alone each night, praying that when I go to sleep,
Things can only get better, they don't.

Fighting bombs, guns everywhere, it's so unfair
And it never goes away, never.
I wish the pain would stop, I can't understand smiles or love.
In this world of devastation and discrimination
People are so thoughtless, so selfish,
Everyone is numb.

I can only imagine this, but for many other people in our world,
It's so *deadly* true.

Katie Crooks (14)
Cambridge House Grammar School

The Night

The night surrounds us all
Watches as it creeps and crawls
As the night silently falls
As the light begins to wane
The silence is deadly, it numbs the brain

I watch as the day becomes night
It swallows up all of the light
The air becomes cold
I think I must be getting old

And as I sit, something draws near
And I fear for my life
It turns out to be a stray cat
And I think that's that.

Hugh King (13)
Cambridge House Grammar School

Dogs

Cute dogs, cuddly dogs
Big dogs, small dogs
Friendly dogs, yappy dogs
Everyone loves dogs

Jack Russells in the fields
Hunting for their meals
Lunchtime will come
Yum! Yum!

Guide dogs for the blind
Are loyal and kind
Help their masters cross the road
And seem to know the Green Cross Code

Spotty Dalmatians
Film sensations
Watch out for Cruella
Woof! Here she comes.

Leanne McAuley (11)
Cambridge House Grammar School

The Underground Train

The underground train,
The underground train,
If you'll permit me to explain,
Is like a busy beetle, black,
That scoots along a silver track;
And, whether it be night or day,
The beetle has to find its way,
Because the only place it's found,
Is deep, deep, deep underground.

John McCrory (13)
Cambridge House Grammar School

What About War?

War is terrible, with so many people dying
Leaving families and loved ones distorted and crying.
War can change everything, some things or nothing.
What's wrong with peace?
Nothing's wrong with peace,
Sometimes we might need war, other times we will not.

Is it right to send people to die in some unknown land,
Or should all these gun fights and aerial onslaughts be banned?
Should the world not be a safe haven for us to relax,
Or maybe the world will turn into a country where rivers are
                                                      red with blood,
What would I choose?
I would choose peace and unity.

Daniel Cummings (13)
Cambridge House Grammar School

December

D ark, damp winter nights
E very house has twinkling lights
C old, yet cheerful people pass
E ach thought of Christmas past
M istletoe and wine to add Christmas cheer
B usy robins seem to have no fear
E vergreen branches laden with snow
R eindeer and presents with fancy bows

Christmas, however, lest we forget is to celebrate
the birth of our Lord.
So let December find us all, happy, healthy
And rejoice in one accord.

Ian Currie (11)
Cambridge House Grammar School

How

Make-up, jewellery and all those things,
Gold, silver, money and rings,
Flowers, lipstick and flashy cars
And everyone acting like they're pop stars.
Big houses, restaurants and cruises on holiday,
Ornaments, mobile phones and big cheques for pay.

But are all these what we really need?
As from more unfortunate people, let their lives be our lead,
Clean water, proper schooling and food to eat,
Others walking dirt tracks with dusty, tired feet.
Little children dying when they're only young,
So many of our delicacies have never touched their tongue.

But what can we do to change their lives?
To help the kids without parents, the men without wives?
Some with no proper clothes to wear,
With all our wealth, you'd think we could share,
With so many different charities helping us to do this,
So children can get good education and other things they might miss.

Wars breaking out and people dying,
Nuclear bombs killing and families crying,
But it doesn't all have to end in sorrow,
For some there is hope for tomorrow.
As there are kind people, who are caring and give,
So others may live just as we here live.

But the question is, what will you do now?
So help and care and not just ask . . . how?

Joanne Fleck (13)
Cambridge House Grammar School

Clouds

All different shapes
Sometimes just circles, sometimes scribbled lines
So fluffy and soft
Like candyfloss in the sky

All different colours
Sometimes pink, sometimes white, sometimes black
So fluffy and soft
Like cotton wool in the sky.

Sophie Scott (11)
Cambridge House Grammar School

I Love The Letter 'L'

The lashing looks of the luscious lipstick
On the lips of the lenient lady,
The lingering taste of a lifeless lemon,
The long lasting light of a lamp
And the lethal jaws on a large lion.
The lemonade spilt on the loaf,
The ladder that has lost a rung,
The lush leaves on the lime tree
And the lanky leaves of a lettuce.

Robyn McCormick (13)
Cambridge House Grammar School

Autumn

A pples dipped in toffee, yum!
U mbrellas at the ready
T rees starting to lose their leaves
U nder leaves, chestnuts lie
M onkey nuts in moderation
N ever does you any harm.

Lisa Magee (12)
Cambridge House Grammar School

Hallowe'en

H is for horror which scares you at night.
A is for apples, all juicy and ripe.
L is for lights which brighten the night.
L is for lanterns which show you the way.
O is for October on an autumn's day.
W is for witches that fly in the sky.
E is for eyes that show you the way.
E is for excitement which fills children with joy.
N is for night sky that scared the little boy.

Kenneth Sproule (11)
Cambridge House Grammar School

October

O wls hoot into the sky
C hildren sing to neighbours by
T he leaves are lying on the ground
O ctober months are very cold
B usy hedgehogs run around
E ating toffee apples
R abbits run into their burrows.

Jonathan McKeown (12)
Cambridge House Grammar School

Autumn

A s I watch out the window, I see the leaves fall,
U nderneath it all, the little hedgehogs crawl,
T he trees are turning bare,
U nbearable to watch, autumn is here, winter is near.
M any little creatures are preparing all their food,
'N ever! I'll never make it through this long, cold winter!' they cry.

Emma McConnell (11)
Cambridge House Grammar School

Autumn

As the leaves begin to fall
I know that autumn is coming soon
I sit up on the high wall
Watching the birds flying below the moon

The pleasant summer is gone
The colours of the flowers have gone to sleep
The mornings are very dark at dawn
Soon Jack Frost will have a peep

Autumn is the sign of Hallowe'en
Time for children to trick or treat
Bonfire flames seem to beam
This is the end of summer's heat.

Sarah McClenaghan (11)
Cambridge House Grammar School

War

War is cruel
War is bad
It makes people like me
Sad
Guns are roaring
Day and night
It gives people like us
A chilling fright
Soldiers are dying
Bombs are flying
It makes us believe that
We should stop crying.

David O'Neill (13)
Cambridge House Grammar School

October

Autumn leaves are falling,
Hallowe'en is here,
When we see witches with pointy hats
And little black cats.

Witches that sit on their broomsticks and fly,
Up high into the night sky
And big, round, orange pumpkins,
With scary faces on them.

Orange and red, all the different colours,
That burst into the night sky

And if you're lucky, you may hear a witch cackling,
Or even better you might see one whirling
Around in the black night sky,
With a cat hanging on for its life!

Rebecca McAllister (12)
Cambridge House Grammar School

Mack's Match

I kicked the ball so very strong
Then I realised I'd done it all wrong
It didn't go near the net at all
But went to one of the defenders small

He hit it back out
And all they did shout
Was . . .
'You've gone and done it again!'

I reckoned I could easily beat the guy at the back
With my great skill I would show who I was - Mack!

Then came my chance to score another
So I ran to the net without any bother
They were cheering me on and then my chance came
I booted it in, a goal to my name!

Jonathan McCabe (11)
Cambridge House Grammar School

Hallowe'en

Hallowe'en is an exciting time,
A time for ghosts and ghouls,
The air is filled with smoky fumes
And children dress up like fools.

The smell of the crackling fireworks,
Makes my tummy tingle,
Animals tucked safely up inside,
As the rest of the neighbourhood mingle.

Rat-a-tat-tat on my friend's door,
Dressed as a witch with my broomstick and more,
I hear a noise and look around,
The dead are walking on the ground.

The dead are white and drained of blood,
Their hearts no beat, their face no smile,
We look in horror as they come our way
And run and run for the next mile.

When the night has passed and my tummy aches,
With apples and candy galore,
I say goodnight to my ghoulish friends,
Go home and close the door . . .

Samantha-Jane Stewart (11)
Cambridge House Grammar School

Autumn

A ll the leaves fall off the trees,
U p with a bang go the fireworks,
T offee apples to eat at Hallowe'en,
U nder the water, dunking for apples,
M oney to be found in the apple tarts,
N ow my bag is full from trick or treat.

Daniel Smyth (11)
Cambridge House Grammar School

Your Horse Year

In the spring after winter
Some horses out to grass
Others in a little longer
Need to be groomed
At night their feed
Then have their sleep
Now time for yours

In the summer many out
Green grass and run wild
A sudden neigh to a friend
Others hear then reply
A buck and a skip
Then eat and eat
Now time for yours

In the autumn the showing over
Grass is getting scarce
Prepare for cooler days
Some sold to other homes
Old friends never leave
Enjoy their lasting comfort
Now time for yours

In the winter Jack Frost arrives
Too cold behind the hedge
A warm stable and dry bed
A friendly voice to hear
Rugged up in style
Then out for exercise
Now time for yours.

Caryn Walker (12)
Cambridge House Grammar School

Events In Autumn

Leaves, leaves everywhere
Golden brown, orange and yellow
Getting ready for the snow

Costumes, costumes everywhere
As it's coming up to Hallowe'en
Many strange things to be seen

Fire, fire everywhere
It's just right
To have on Bonfire Night

Fireworks, fireworks everywhere
Many different colours up high
Flashing and screaming in the sky.

Kayleigh Gregor (12)
Cambridge House Grammar School

Hallowe'en

H owling wolves
A ll around you ghostly sounds
L ove trick or treating
L ike scaring people
O h! The excitement on the ground
W itches fly on broomsticks
E ach of us likes nuts and apples
E vening fireworks with a bang
N othing gets a chance to sleep.

Niall Graham (11)
Cambridge House Grammar School

An Old Man Down The Street

There was an old man down the street
And he was frightful to meet.

His name was Jay
And one day,
His wife said, 'Change your scary ways
Or I'm moving away.'

Then one day he said, 'Hello.'
And I said, 'Go, just go.'
For he looked awfully scary
And his arms were all dirty and hairy.

Then one day he had a bath
And his wife had a terrible laugh,
She said, 'Now you smell much better,
You should write everyone in the street a letter.'

Ever since they got that letter,
Everyone likes him a whole lot better.

Joey McCann (11)
Cambridge House Grammar School

The Lady By The Road

The lady by the road, roams the streets,
begging people to give her money for a feast.

The lady by the road, has no car that goes by speed power,
or any shelter from the cold winter.

The lady by the road, cries at night,
hoping tomorrow will be more of a delight.

The lady by the road, has no family
to depend on when things go wrong.

Naomi Redmond (12)
Cambridge House Grammar School

Hallowe'en

The ghosts went boo
The bats when eek eek
I couldn't sleep
Then I heard a Greek
So I took a little peak

I looked out the window
I saw a wicked witch
She was singing at a very loud pitch
Then I saw her fly
While she screeched bye bye

I heard people say trick or treat
Then they began to eat
At the bottom of the stairs
There was layers and layers of sweets
Everybody began to eat

We were all very full
Then we went outside to trick or treat
We got a lot of sweets
That we sadly couldn't eat.

Amy McCosh (11)
Cambridge House Grammar School

Winter On The Way

Autumn arrives far too soon
Letting us know winter is on the way
Leaves change colour and fall to the ground
Children have to wrap up to play

The days get short and the nights longer
At home is where we choose to stay
As winter approaches and it gets colder
Jack Frost is surely on his way.

Jason Ross (12)
Cambridge House Grammar School

Autumn

Autumn is the time of year,
When leaves fall off the trees,
We always know when it is here,
There's no more summer breeze.

The wind and rain have come once more,
We'd like to stay in bed,
We do not know what lies in store,
In the blustery days ahead.

The days grow short, the nights grow long,
Day blends into night,
Soon we'll hear the robin's song,
When other birds have taken flight.

Horse chestnuts are so big and round,
Children have a ball,
Rummaging along the ground,
Waiting for them to fall.

In autumn we have Hallowe'en,
With costumes and scary faces,
Ghosts and ghouls can all be found,
If you look in the right places.

We all enjoy autumn,
It's a very colourful season,
There's lots and lots to do and see,
To dislike it we'd need good reason.

For seasons come and seasons go,
The next one soon will bring the snow,
So to conclude I'd like to say,
Enjoy this lovely autumn day.

James Watt (11)
Cambridge House Grammar School

I Wish I Was . . .

I'm a house dog, a lazy dog that lies by the fire all day,
I'm a friendly dog, a quiet dog, people love to be my owner,
I'm a meek dog, a sleek dog that gets two meals set down each day,
I'm a tame dog, a sane dog that gets cared for by my owner.

I wish I was a crazy dog, not a lazy dog that plays about
                                        day and night,
I wish I was a rough dog, a tough dog that hunts for my own food,
I wish I was a wild dog who would keep humans awake all night,
I wish I was in a gang of dogs so we could lead the neighbourhood.

Kerry Ritchie (13)
Downshire School

House Cat

I'm a sleek cat, a house cat, licking all my fur
I'm a big cat, a fat cat, sleeping on my mat
I'm a clean cat, a mean cat, chasing tiny mice
I love to lie and sleep all day and wander round the house

I'm not an alley cat, I'm not a scruffy stray
I'm not a wild cat, I just like to laze all day
I'm not a greedy cat or one who will steal food
I am just a sleepy cat, I'd sleep all day if I could.

Victoria Hawkins (13)
Downshire School

Bad Cat

I'm a mad cat, a bad cat, chasing silly mice,
I'm a lazy cat, a crazy cat and I'm not very nice,
Don't come any closer or I'll give you my lice.

I'm a sneaky cat, a freaky cat and I am so cool,
I'm a scary cat, a hairy cat, no I'm not a fool,
But I'm not like the other cats chasing balls of wool.

Heather Irwin (13)
Downshire School

A Recipe For Happiness

An ounce of sleeping
A slice of cake
Mix with care
With a squeeze of rain
Half a cup of fun, fun, fun
And a large tablespoon of science
A freshly picked computer
Add the badminton
Stir in a TV
Bake slowly
Then add a pinch of tennis
And a sprinkle of clothes
Pour in a PlayStation 2
And a good helping of cats and dogs
Hey presto
The recipe is done.

Gemma Boyd (11)
Downshire School

The Great White Shark

I'm the big kind, the fierce kind,
The cunning kind of shark;
I'm a bad shark, a mad shark,
Scaring silly men;
I love to watch them, to study them, to eat them.

My way is the best way,
The only way for me;
Drifting from coast to coast,
Searching for my next victim;
I am the great white shark.

Scott Loudon (14)
Downshire School

A Recipe For Happiness!

One stone of my mobile phone
Four kg of throwing my dog a bone
Two pounds of feeling the wind in my face
Half a teaspoon of playing bass
A wage of my loving family
And a dash of growing things
Add a pinch of horror films
To spice it up at this stage
A tablespoon of taking my pet out of that cage
A gram of shopping for expensive clothes
Six ounces of watching Homer going to Moe's
Add a dash of my computer and
A handful of art
Stir well and leave to set
And this will complete my recipe.

Lyndsey Cooke (11)
Downshire School

A Recipe For Happiness

An ounce of art
With a sprinkle of science
Add a pinch of TV
With a squeeze of swimming
Mix up well
A splash of music
Half a cup of tennis
Bake slowly with a bounce of the trampoline
A tablespoon of shopping
With a dash of holidays
A slice of birthday parties
With a game from the PlayStation
And that's the recipe done.

Lynsey Cowan (11)
Downshire School

My Recipe For Happiness

A gram of scoring goals in football,
A piece of playing all my games on the PS1,
With half a cup of visiting my granny,
Also a slice of Sunday dinner, yum, yum,
Mix well with a weekend chilli ribs and chips,
Add a freshly made video,
Stir in with a bag of chocolate peanuts,
Bake with watching the music channels,
Serve with a helping of swimming
And there you are - my recipe's done.

Jonathan Campbell (11)
Downshire School

The Sounds Of Our House

I hear a dog barking outside,
Darren's music going loud.
The washing machine going round and round,
The fridge joins in the sound.
Ding, ding, goes the microwave,
The TV is so loud.
People laughing on a comedy show.

Stacey McClelland (12)
Mount Gilbert Community College

Belfast

Belfast, Belfast is my home,
Every day I love to roam,
Lots of shops all around,
Fantastic places to be found,
You may say it is no good,
But I would say you could
Come and see for yourself.

Amy Coulter (12)
Mount Gilbert Community College

Spitting

He spits on the table,
He spits on the floor,
He spits on other people,
Through the open door.

He kicks a football,
Up and down the street.
He thinks he's David Beckham,
But he's got two left feet.

He shouts instead of talking,
He likes a lot of noise.
The TV always has to be up loud
My mum says - *Boys will be boys!*

Lee Brown (13)
Mount Gilbert Community College

The Sound Of Silence

A car speeding down the hill,
Dad strumming on his guitar.
The TV making funny sounds,
The football bouncing on the ground.

Boys and girls shouting out in the street,
The ice cream man playing funny tunes.
A door creaking,
The tap leaking,
My mum and dad speaking,
My sounds of silence.

Mark Osborne (13)
Mount Gilbert Community College

No Sleep Tonight Again!

Rioting
Lots of noise
Thump, crash, bang
Up that street
Round the corner
Angry voices
Children crying
People could be dying
Can't sleep at night
Adults passing down their hatred
Sticks, bricks and stones flying everywhere
Police have put cameras up but will it stop?
Why are we still fighting?
Why does this have to be?
Can't we be friends?
We are not so different
Why are we not allowed to be friends?
We both like hanging about with our mates having a laugh
Why can't we laugh together?

Leah Smyth (13)
Mount Gilbert Community College

The Background

When I am with my friends sometimes
I feel as if I am in the background

I feel like the invisible man
I feel as if I am in the background

People think I am fine
But by far they are wrong

I am in the background
Always in the background.

Matthew Evans (13)
Mount Gilbert Community College

Fame

Is it really everything?
Privacy is seldom.
Press at your door
Waiting for any news
To feed to the public.
Caring about nothing
Or no one.
Never caring who they hurt.
Vicious rumours spread about.
Fame?
No thanks!

Danielle Garvin (14)
Mount Gilbert Community College

All Hallows Eve

Children getting ready,
For parties and trick or treating,
Banging on the door,
Dropping candy on the floor.

Ghostly beings in the light,
Children's faces full of fright,
Out they hold their hands,
While sweets appear to fill their palms.

Stories of horror,
Children tremor,
They're crying,
From stories of dying.

At this night's end,
Check under your bed,
You might find something unforeseen,
Like a monster looming and mean.

James O'Boyle (11)
St Malachy's College, Belfast

Christ

Christ is very special,
In every way for me,
Christ is very special,
For all my family.
It was very light,
On Jesus' birth night.
The star was very bright,
The star lit up the night.
The wise men saw the star,
They travelled very far.
The shepherds brought sheep
And lay them on a sheet.
When the angel came in the air,
Jesus became the heir.
They stayed in a barn
And it was very old and cold.

Christopher Roberts (12)
St Malachy's College, Belfast

Henrik Larsson

Henrik Larsson is the king of kings,
Every time he scores the Celtic fans sing,
He was cheap, only 650 grand,
You would think he came from the promised land.

When I go to see him play,
He never makes me sad on that day.
1, 2, 3 go in,
He's the best player there's ever been.

James Christian (12)
St Malachy's College, Belfast

The Grim Reaper

One night I was peering out of the window
And I saw a black dressed man.
There were no noises of any kind but the sound of a rolling can.
I shined a torch on the man
And the light shined right back.
The man had a shiny scythe in his hand and a big black old sack.
I shouted, 'Mummy! Mummy!' and 'Daddy! Daddy!'
But no one was in.
The man slipped into the house then I fell and hit my shin,
'Ow! Ow!' I shouted but no one would hear me anyway.

Footsteps came up the stairs,
I then sprinted under the bed.
I knew the man was after me, he probably wanted my head.
He came into the room that I was in.
He pushed everything down even the bin.
The man looked under the bed, I was in great fright.
The man said, 'I am the Grim Reaper,'
On that horrible scary night.

Brendan Garland (11)
St Malachy's College, Belfast

The Sea

The sea houses lots of animals,
Some of them are mammals like
Seals and dolphins.
There are lots of boats on the water
And there are some sunken ones below.
In the winter the sea is as cold as ice.
In the summer the water is as blue as the sky.
When it is windy the sea sounds like a hungry giant.

Conor Lawlor (12)
St Malachy's College, Belfast

Bad Fog

One day I was out for a jog,
There was a bad fog,
But there was no need for alarm,
It wouldn't do me any harm.

As I ran on, the fog didn't get better,
The rain came on and I got much wetter.
I was going to turn back and go home,
But I thought it would be better to wander and roam.

I'm completely lost, I can't go back,
It is all my fault, it's intelligence I lack.
The fog shows no mercy, it's a raging beast,
I can't go home, I think I'll head east.

I can see some lights ahead, I'm going to win the fight,
When I said I would make it, I knew I was right!
The lights are bigger, closer they come,
My head is sore, my fingers are numb.

I can't give up, I can't give in,
Despite the rain pelting off my skin.
I'm there! *Yes!* I won the fight,
I said I'd win, I knew I was right!

The place I'm in is a hotel,
I'm into Heaven and out of Hell.
I'll contact home, I think I'll phone,
I'll ask my mum to take me home.

James Wilson (11)
St Malachy's College, Belfast

The Rich Bee

The rich bee had lots of money
He got it all by selling honey
But one day this all changed
The day when bee got engaged
His darling girl was not as she seemed
She wasn't the way he always dreamed
Bee found out that night
When he and his girl had a terrible fight
She took him to court for custody of money
The money he made with all *his* honey
She won the money
And found it funny
That was a waste of all his honey
And that's what happens if you have loads of money.

Michael O'Reilly (12)
St Malachy's College, Belfast

Enly Avenue

I'm lost in a neighbourhood I do not know,
Its name's Gorgleville, one street I noticed was Enly Avenue,
Enly Avenue held many surprises, as I was soon to learn.
The roofs of the houses were high and low where mortal footsteps
feared to go.

I walked down the street not knowing what I'd done,
But I soon found out because what I saw made me run.
It was a ghostly image with horns on its head
and it said to me, 'You're dead!'
I ran far from that street and only yesterday did I return to Gorgleville
and as the sun shone I saw that Gorgleville was
gone!

Conor Curran (11)
St Malachy's College, Belfast

Robot Wars

They crash and smash,
In the arena wars.
Often they are bashed,
Against the walls.
The names we know,
Pussycat, Hypnodisc and Chaos 2,
Robots to name a few.

All in a spin hoping,
They all will win.
Here's Chaos 2,
The champ of them all.
He holds the cup,
He has beaten them all.

They're baying for blood,
He knows if he fails,
They'll smash and crash him against the walls.
Bolts Metal, your heart all gone,
No more chance in Robot Wars.

There's mayhem and carnage,
From Sgt Bash, house robots all waiting to smash.
Matilda will take you for
A different dance.

No song or a prayer
Will save you from him.
Sir Killalot's lance, so strong and long,
Crunching pinchers are a work of art.
Will send fear into your very heart,
Tears just save them, you're almost gone.

Smell the fear, there's blood and sweat,
Gone is the hope as you're on fire.
Burnt-out shell, month of waste,
As you're no longer in the race.

David Brennan (11)
St Malachy's College, Belfast

Into The Deep

Into the deep where nobody goes,
The mysterious place that no one knows.
We don't know what's down there,
But when we find something we know it's rare.

We really want to know some new things,
The good information that it brings.
The sea is being polluted and that is bad,
The destruction and pollution would make you sad.

There are loads of stuff including some fish and sharks,
Some people think that sharks attack at dark.
A man that lived on the beach and had no job,
He found something weird and it was called *The Blob.*

The sea is so furious that it swallows up some boats
And the shipwrecks all they do is float,
The waves that come off the sea,
They are scary enough to make you flee.

That's what I've got to say about the deep,
But do take care before you leap.

Michael Briers (11)
St Malachy's College, Belfast

Dawn To Dusk

In the morning the sun makes it climb,
It slowly rises into the sky,
Like a rocket going off in the distance in slow motion,
From the black night to a bright day,
Like a lamp being switched on,
This is dawn!

During the day the sun moves slowly,
It seems to be lying there motionless,
It's like staring at a clock,
As if it won't move while you are looking.
It looks as if it won't go,
But it is going, you just wouldn't think so.

In the night the sun begins to fall,
It slowly descends below the ground,
Like a plane landing from the sky,
Moving from a bright day to a dark night.
Like a lamp being switched off,
This is dusk!

Daniel Thompson (11)
St Malachy's College, Belfast

The Dark Streets Of Belfast

The lonely streets of Belfast are dark, cold and wet.
The streetlights are like a row of long flickering eyes casting
Their evil eye on the surrounding
Community houses and bedsits.
The gates of the yards are like huge
Mouths with their giant
Sharp teeth waiting to gobble you up
As you try to enter your *own* home.
The tiny play-parks lie empty with only a
Tiny fire lit by the hoods.
The shadows on the wall look as if they are
Going to chase me to my death,
Not even the local pub McRackens is open
On this dark, cold and wet night.
The streets are like my head, empty and cold,
I feel like the shadows are digging my grave here.

Fionntan O'Connor (12)
St Malachy's College, Belfast

The Library

Books that are funny,
Books that are sad,
Books that are funky,
They make me mad.

There are books on cars,
Books on flowers,
Books ten centimetres thick,
To read them would take hours.

There are books on'The Simpsons'
Books on 'Where's Wally?',
Books on fishing,
Reading them makes me jolly.

Aron Fields (11)
St Malachy's College, Belfast

Hallowe'en

Hallowe'en is near,
Do you dare to peer
Through the hole in the door?
The sight will make your eyes sore.

There were goblins and ghouls,
Vampires and flying tools,
Werewolves and witches
And cats stuck in ditches.
There were also bats
That only ate cats.

So when Hallowe'en is near,
It is a bad idea to peer
Through the hole in the door,
The sight made my eyes sore.

Daniel Clarke (11)
St Malachy's College, Belfast

The Wind

You think back on your life, thinking why the wind is out to get you,
You feel that the wind is like a paramilitary group coming
                                        out to kill you.
Then comes silence. You are more frightened now than
                                you were before. *Bang!*
The trees bang off your upstairs window! You close your eyes
                        and hope everything will be alright.

You get up and look out the window. It is bright and everything
                                is surprisingly calm.
There are trees lying on the ground. The wind has killed
                                these poor creatures.
Somehow you have survived this time, but it's winter,
Be prepared!

Padraig McGlinchey (12)
St Malachy's College, Belfast

The Black Rider

It was just a normal stormy night,
That gave me an unexpected fright.
A black cat was sitting by my window,
Suddenly from behind it came a red fiery glow.
The cat became engulfed in flame,
Surely I would get the blame.

Suddenly a figure rose from the ground,
His steed a giant hellhound.
The figure came running towards the house,
I got the feeling that I was just a little mouse.

The figure crashed through the window,
There it was again, that fiery red glow!
The figure jumped off his steed,
I ran as fast as I could, with much speed.

I running, running! Then I fell!
The figure walked up with his hound of Hell.
He drew his sword which glinted in the moonlight,
His horrible hellhound gave me a bite.

Then I got away from the figure of doom
And awoke in my bed in my cosy little room.
So that's the story of my fright,
On that dreaded Hallowe'en night.

Mark Keenan (12)
St Malachy's College, Belfast

Inside The House

Inside the house is cosy and warm
Out in the street there is a storm
On the road there has grown a river
I hear a screech, it makes me shiver
A car has crashed, that's no surprise
With fog like this, the clouded eyes . . .

I went outside and there I could see
Nothing that was around me
I tumbled over the garden fence
It's hard to see, this fog is so thick and dense
I decided to go back inside
To wait for the storm to subside

On the way back all I could hear
Was the wind howling in my ear
When I got inside and closed the door
I ran across the wooden floor
I sat beside the fire, in the chair
Until that storm was over I sat there
Inside the house was cosy and warm
Out in the street there was a storm.

Joseph Fanning (12)
St Malachy's College, Belfast

A Rainy Night

Water, water everywhere but not a drop to drink,
Rainclouds hang everywhere,
Little droplets hang from my hair,
The rain begins to get angry,
It lashes from the heavens,
Like an army of daggers falling all around.
I run as fast as I can,
But my coat is holding me down,
The wetness like an anchor sticking me to the ground.
My hands hunched in my pockets,
I also have in there,
My rainbow chews and strawberry lockets.
The cars rushing past like hungry cheetahs,
Their tyres squeak, longing to stop.
I finally reach my warm, cosy home
And waiting there is my mum on the phone,
When I get in she shouts with glee,
'I am so glad to see you home.
Come and sit down and warm yourself through,
With my lovely and gorgeous home-made stew.'

Christopher Boy (12)
St Malachy's College, Belfast

Who's Out There?

I'm in my house watching TV,
But I feel like someone else is watching, watching me!
As I look out of my window, I see bright eyes,
Friend or foe?
What is it?

I'm in my house worrying,
What's out there? What is this thing?
It sits out there, not moving,
Not saying a word.
What is it?

I'm in my house, frozen still.
I build up my courage and confront the beast.
It comes out of its hiding space,
It comes right at me.
What is it?

I'm in my house laughing,
The beast was an owl.
It was an owl.

Alan Kennedy (12)
St Malachy's College, Belfast

All In The Mind

Oh my God!
It's like the Antrim Road, it's so long!
And I don't like those trees; anything could be in there!
There are no lights and it's really dark.
I'll just have to walk quickly.

What was that?
There's someone behind me,
Now they're in the trees and they're running,
Running in front of me.
They've stopped.

Just keep walking, I'll be alright!
I think I'm past him now,
But he's still there, isn't he?
Yeah he is and he has got a knife!
Just . . . keep . . . walking . . . don't look back!

Is that it?
That was shorter than I thought!
And where's your man with the knife?
Was he ever really there?
Nah . . . I don't think he was!

Michael Monaghan (12)
St Malachy's College, Belfast

Revenge For My House!

My one possession, memory and soul,
Is being demolished by ugly, heartless men.
They bring tools, diggers and more,
But little do they know that I am immortal,
I shall obliterate them all.

So let them come!
My house is what they come for,
To overthrow my only possession,
But I won't let them!

I shall call upon the walls,
To draw them into eternal darkness,
Where their skeletons will rot and fester!

I shall call upon the iron nails,
To blind these selfish men.
For they do not deserve to see,
What lies before them.

I shall call upon the floorboards,
To draw them towards the Earth,
I shall make it so they will stifle,
Never to extinguish my fire-like memory of my house.

They *will* leave after this,
Or I will do much worse.
So let them come
And they will feel my wrath!

Kevin Glover (12)
St Malachy's College, Belfast

Summer

Summer holidays arrive at last
And now school is in the past,
Lots of free time to do as I please,
I jump on my bike and feel the breeze.

The sun is shining and the air smells sweet
And Granny said, 'You're in for a treat,'
We're going away to somewhere hot,
But where we're going I know not.

My summer holiday was a blast,
I thought it would last and last,
But now I'm back at home,
I can tell my friends about it on the phone.

In summer I play sports with my dad
And in some sports I'm really bad.
This summer was fun but now it is done,
But bad memories I have none.

Now the summer is over,
I'm being dropped to school in my mum's Rover,
The summer holidays were cool,
But now I am back at school!

Ben McCusker (11)
St Malachy's College, Belfast

The Rain And The Sun

One day the rain and the sun had a big fight,
They hit each other with all of their might.
This went on for months, days and nights
And gave the world below them a massive fright.

Through the day it rained and the sun shone
And at night it seemed as though they had gone.
But in the morning you could see them again,
Each of them was going through a lot of pain.

Then all of a sudden a rainbow came out,
A man below started to shout.
'Look at those colours, there's blue and there's white,
Rain and sun why must you fight?'

The rain and the sun learned how to love,
It must have been a gift from above.
So the sun and the rain became good friends
And that is how the story ends.

Odhrán Livingstone (11)
St Malachy's College, Belfast

Stalker

What does he want? she thinks to herself.
Who is he? she thinks to herself.
He's coming to get her and when he does,
He's going to scare her to death.

A man with a dark clock searches for her,
She doesn't know what he wants, I do.
He wants his baby back and he's gonna get it,
Now she waits at the window, shotgun handy.

The wind blows against the window of a house,
300 miles from the world, 300 miles from safety.
The darkness is hard and scary, she can't see,
Her baby waits upstairs, for now.

Morning will come soon, easier to see,
He doesn't know I'm here, she thinks, she thinks.
Morning came, for most people, not for her,
For he got his baby back, just as I said.

Michael Russell (12)
St Malachy's College, Belfast

They Are Coming

They are coming to get you.
They are coming to find you.
They are coming to kill you.
Don't let them get you.

Lock the doors,
Get the gun,
Hide under the bed,
Don't let them get you.

Pack up your things,
Let's go, they are coming.
Coming to find you.
Don't let them get you.

Run, run and keep on running.
Run away from them.
Don't let them get you.

Chris Murray (13)
St Malachy's College, Belfast